University Entrance

by Jonathan Watts and Cora Saint

University Entrance

CONTENTS

University Entrance

Jonathan Watts and Cora Saint

Edited by Janita Clamp

Series Editor: Emma Bartley

Published by
Gresham Books Limited
The Carriage House
Ningwood Manor
Ningwood
Isle of Wight
PO30 4NJ

Main Cover Image: Rawpixel Ltd/iStock/Thinkstock

ISBN 978-0-946095-61-2

Design by Words & Pictures
Typesetting and layout by Fiona Jerome
Printed in the UK

HEARING BACK

WHAT HAPPENS NEXT?

UNIVERSITY LIFE

Introduction

As a Principal, with a responsibility for sixth form students, I welcome this excellent publication on University Entrance, which will be an immense support not only to students and parents in understanding the UCAS process but also to leaders of Sixth Form schools and colleges—and to teachers in guiding their students in their university and higher education applications. This book gives a full and comprehensive overview of all that is involved in applying to university or other higher education institutions.

Being a student in the sixth form is a special and exciting time in one's educational journey, offering new opportunities and challenges and broadening one's horizons. The subjects which students choose to study in sixth form can be the first step onto a particular career path, but career paths are widening and at this time it is so important to be well informed and to choose what is right for each individual.

Choosing whether to apply to university is likely to be one of the most important decisions students will have had to make at this time in their lives. In my fifteen years of headship I have always encouraged all students who have the academic ability to continue their studies at university. Not only will their lives be enriched by the experience of studying a subject they enjoy in real depth, meeting new people and developing life long friendships but obtaining a degree will open up many more career opportunities for them. I tell my students that a degree opens the door to further study and to life long learning.

As parents, we play a key role in supporting our children to make considered and responsible decisions in their UCAS applications. As a parent of four children, one in her first year at university and three who have successfully graduated, I have first hand experience of the pressure on students during this time of applying to university. I believe it is important for parents to share the UCAS process and to discuss the merits of particular courses and universities. Parents need to help their sons and daughters to realise what is important to them in their further study and indeed what is important to them in life. The love, support and encouragement parents provide their children at this vital time in their lives is paramount to helping them to be happy as well as to be successful.

I trust that this book will guide parents to help their children make the correct choice of career path, and to be successful in their UCAS application. I would recommend all schools and colleges with a sixth form to place multiple copies of this book in their libraries.

John McParland
Principal, The John Wallis Church of England Academy

About the Authors

Jonathan Watts spent the majority of his long teaching career at Benenden School, where he was Head of History and Politics as well as Scholars' Mentor, with a special responsibility for advising students on Oxbridge application.

Cora Saint has a PGDip in careers guidance with distinction. She previously worked as Head of Careers at Benenden School, before moving on to her current role as Director of Development and a member of the Senior Management Team.

WHAT IS UCAS?

If your son or daughter is in the Sixth Form you will hear 'UCAS' mentioned frequently. Now's a good time to get to know the facts behind the acronym.

Digital Vision/THINKSTOCK

UCAS (Universities and Colleges Admissions Service) is the organisation that processes applications for undergraduate degree courses at the vast majority of universities in the UK. All students applying to study at a UK university must do so through UCAS; this includes students from the EU and international students. UCAS is a non-governmental, not-for-profit organisation. It is funded by the fees it charges for applications (currently between £12 and £23).

Although processing higher education applications is the core activity of UCAS, the organisation also provides a great deal of information about courses, post-16 options, careers and apprenticeships. Video guides on subjects such as 'Preparing for higher education', 'The journey of an application' and 'Finance and funding', live blogs and webchats are used to address application queries using a range of social media.

Music, dance and drama courses

In the case of music, dance or drama courses, some but not all applications are made through UCAS. This depends on the type of institution offering the course. If the course is provided by a conservatoire (these offer specialist professional training) there is a separate application facility: UCAS Conservatoires (formerly CUKAS).

Postgraduate courses

UCAS also provides an application service for all full-time postgraduate courses through UKPASS (the UK Postgraduate Application and Statistical Service) and for postgraduate teacher training applications through UCAS Teacher Training. ■

THIS MAY HELP

Parent Guides, which cover the key stages of the undergraduate application process, are produced each year and are available from the UCAS website.

g-stockstudio/iStock/THINKSTOCK

HOW DOES UCAS WORK?

UCAS makes the university application process much simpler, by communicating with the universities on your child's behalf.

UCAS applications are made online through UCAS Apply. As soon as UCAS Apply goes live, your son or daughter can register and make a start on completing their application. There are seven sections to be completed: Personal Details, Additional Information (not required for international applications), Student Finance, Choices, Education, Employment and Personal Statement. The sections that require most research, thought and work are Choices and the Personal Statement.

Applicants may put down up to five university choices. In the case of Medicine, Dentistry, Veterinary Medicine and Veterinary Science courses, they may select only four for their chosen subject but can add a fifth choice in a different subject. This fifth choice is encouraged as a sensible 'back up' given the similar and highly competitive entry requirements for all medical, dentistry and veterinary schools.

Most students apply to UCAS through their school or college. When they submit their application in this way it will first go to the school or college for the reference and predicted grades to be added. This is also an opportunity for the school or college to review a student's application and

A STUDENT SPEAKS

THE UCAS PROCESS

"UCAS Apply took a while to get the hang of, and at first it seemed very complex, but it became much clearer with some advice from friends, the Internet, and my school. The hardest part was spending hours fiddling with the character count of the Personal Statement, removing commas and quotation marks where possible to squeeze it in!"

Sophie, taking a gap year before Exeter University

moodboard/THINKSTOCK

advise them accordingly if changes are necessary. The school or college will then forward the application to UCAS.

Independent applications may also be made by those, such as home-schooled students, who are not affiliated to a school or college. In this case, applicants should add the details of their referee and UCAS will contact them to upload a reference to the application before it can be submitted by the candidate.

UCAS accepts applications from September and many universities will start to make offers from this time. All applications made within the deadline are given equal consideration; starting the process as soon as possible allows your son or daughter the maximum time to submit a strong application early in the cycle but does not confer any advantage.

Once an application has been submitted to UCAS, it will be checked and the Personal Statement is reviewed to ensure that it has not been copied. This can take up to 48 hours. The application is then sent to all the universities and colleges chosen. UCAS will also email your son or daughter to confirm receipt of their application and to explain how they can follow the progress of their application through UCAS Track. The institutions will not be aware at this stage of your son or daughter's other course or university choices. ■

Ryan McVey/Photodisc/THINKSTOCK

The university application process is all about deadlines and dates: external deadlines from UCAS, internal deadlines from schools and, finally, exam results, confirmation and Clearing.

WHAT DATES DO I NEED FOR MY DIARY?

The key dates in the UCAS application process follow this general pattern. Specific dates for each application cycle are confirmed by UCAS around March. If an application is received after the deadline, it will be forwarded to the universities but there is no obligation for them to consider it; for international applicants, many universities offer extended deadlines and students should check with their chosen universities for the relevant date.

Schools and colleges often set their own internal UCAS deadlines, leaving time for staff to review applications and offer advice.

Year 12

Make a start

Most students visit university open days during the summer term of Year 12, and these will be much more useful if your child has a clear idea of what they want to study: indeed, quite a number of open days have subject-specific elements. A decision made before the end of Year 12 will enable your child to work constructively on their Personal Statement during the summer, and undertake work experience or wider reading which will enhance their application.

The online application system, UCAS Apply, goes live in May. Applicants may then register and begin their application.

Mid-September

You may now press 'send'

Applications to UCAS are now open. Most universities begin making offers as soon as applications come in.

15th October (6pm UK time)

Deadline for medics and Oxbridge

Deadline for submission of applications to the Universities of Oxford and Cambridge. Also for applications to Medicine, Dentistry, Veterinary Medicine and Veterinary Science courses at all institutions.

15th January (6pm UK time)

Deadline for (nearly) everyone else

Deadline for submission of applications to all courses, with the exception of those with a 15th October deadline and some art and design courses which have a 24th March deadline.

February

Act now if you've changed your mind

UCAS Extra opens. This service enables students to apply for alternative courses if they hold no offers for their first five choices or they wish to decline any offers they have received.

March

Some art and design deadlines

Deadline for submission of applications to art and design courses, with the exception of those with a 15th January deadline.

May/June

Have you RSVPd?

Deadline for your son or daughter to reply to their university offers. Applicants will be advised of their reply date once they have received decisions from all their universities. Reply dates differ so it is important that they check their own reply date in Track.

30th June (6pm UK time)

Last chance saloon

Deadline for receipt of all applications. Applications received after this date will be placed automatically into Clearing and applicants will be required to contact the universities directly to be considered.

Early July (6pm UK time on deadline date)

No more Extra

UCAS Extra closes.

Early July

IB results

International Baccalaureate (IB) results are published and university places confirmed.

Early August

Scottish results

Scottish Qualifications Authority (SQA) results are published, university places are confirmed and Scottish Clearing vacancy information is released.

Mid-August

Today's the day

GCE A level, Pre-U and Advanced Diploma results are released, university places are confirmed and Clearing vacancy information is released.

Mid to late August

Want to trade up?

Adjustment opens: if your son or daughter has met and exceeded the conditions of their Firm choice offer (the first choice they have accepted), they may look for an alternative course using the Adjustment facility whilst holding their original Firm choice place. There is a time restriction applied and they must make contact with universities directly to ask if there are any places available through Adjustment.

31st August

Settle everything

Final date for any remaining university offer conditions to be met. Adjustment ends.

September

Last call

Last date for receipt of applications for entry the following year.

End September

All clear

UCAS Clearing vacancy search facility closes. Choices may still be added and applicants accepted through Clearing until mid-October.

20 October

The deadline for adding Clearing choices and universities or colleges accepting Clearing applicants. ■

Mike Watson/moodboard/THINKSTOCK

dolgachov/iStock/THINKSTOCK

WHAT DOES A DEGREE COST?

The cost of a university education is often a cause of concern. Some prospective students and their parents worry about how they will finance and repay the significant expense involved.

Every UK student has access to student finance from the government to help them pay for the cost of their undergraduate education. The type of finance available depends on where in the UK your son or daughter is living when they first apply for a student loan but generally there will be financial support available to meet tuition fee costs and living costs.

THIS MAY HELP

Student finance arrangements differ according to where a student normally lives and where they are planning to study. Details of the precise funding available for students resident in England, Scotland, Wales, Northern Ireland and the EU, together with repayment arrangements can be found on the appropriate government websites.

Tuition Fee Loans are also available to EU students planning to study in the UK. Loans are provided by the Student Loans Company, a government-owned organisation.

At present (April 2016), loans are repayable only when your son or daughter has finished their studies and is earning over £21,000 p.a. if they are from England or Wales, or £17,495 if they are from Scotland or Northern Ireland. Loans are written off 25 years after your son or daughter becomes eligible to repay (35 years in Scotland). Repayment is made through the tax system: the Student Loans Company notifies employers and repayments are deducted automatically from taxable income. These amount to 9% of any earnings above the relevant threshold. If your son or daughter is self-employed they need to indicate on their tax return that they have a student loan and HM Revenue & Customs will advise what they are liable to pay. If they are living outside the UK, payments are made directly to the Student Loans Company.

Tuition Fee Loans

Tuition fees vary between universities, although maximum levels have been imposed for non-private institutions. The levels are dependent on where a student is normally resident and where they are planning to study. Tuition Fee Loans are paid directly to the university or college so your son or daughter will not have access to the funds.

The Tuition Fee Loan covers the full cost of tuition fees (although Wales provides a combination of

THIS MAY HELP

Information on student finance and repayment can be found on the Student Loans Company and appropriate government websites.

STUDENT'S COUNTRY OF RESIDENCE	STUDYING IN ENGLAND	STUDYING IN SCOTLAND	STUDYING IN WALES	STUDYING IN NORTHERN IRELAND
ENGLAND	UP TO £9,000	UP TO £9,000	UP TO £9,000	UP TO £9,000
SCOTLAND	UP TO £9,000	No fee	UP TO £9,000	UP TO £9,000
WALES	UP TO £9,000	UP TO £9,000	UP TO £3,810	UP TO £9,000
NORTHERN IRELAND	UP TO £9,000	UP TO £9,000	UP TO £9,000	UP TO £3,805
EU	UP TO £9,000	No fee	UP TO £3,810	UP TO £3,805

loan and non-repayable grant). The maximum rate a university or college can charge for tuition is £9,000 p.a. for full-time courses. Loans to cover fees for private university courses are currently capped at £6,000 p.a. but raising them to the £9,000 threshold is under discussion.

Maintenance Loans

Maintenance Loans are available to full-time UK students and are used towards living costs, including accommodation, food, travel, household bills and course materials. There are different levels of loan available dependent on where the student attends university, household income, and where they live during the course of their studies—for example, are they going to be living at home, in London (where costs are deemed to be higher) or spending a year of a UK university course studying abroad.

THIS MAY HELP

The tuition fees for each course are published on university and college websites, and this information can also be found on the Fees and Finance tab using the UCAS course search facility.

Loans are paid directly to the student's bank account in three instalments at the beginning of each term (or weekly during term time in Scotland).

Additional funding

Further financial support from the government in the form of grants is available for students in particular circumstances, such as those with disabilities or from low income families. This type of funding does not need to be repaid. Maintenance grants are not available to new full-time students in England.

Many universities also provide scholarships, which are also not repayable. It is important to check with the universities your son or daughter is considering, to establish what funding support may be available. ▶

IN THE KNOW

"Student finance applications take around six weeks to be processed, so it's important for students to apply for their funding as early as possible. Even students who don't have a confirmed place on a course yet should still apply, using the details of the course they're most likely to study, as this can always be changed or cancelled later if circumstances change. Applying early means that students will know what they'll be entitled to for the year, which will help with planning their accommodation and their budgets, as well as ensuring that their funding is available at the start of the academic year."

STUDENT LOANS COMPANY

THIS MAY HELP

Scholarship opportunities can also be identified using the Scholarship Search website.

Making a Student Finance application

Applications are made online and can take up to six weeks to process. The application process opens in the spring preceding university entry. The application requires information both from prospective students and their parents; once a student registers, their parents receive their own account so they can complete information regarding income levels.

There are application deadlines in place for each region to ensure applications can be processed and funds made available in time for the beginning of the academic year. These can be checked on the individual websites. Students are required to apply in each year of their studies.

Interest costs

Interest on the Tuition and Maintenance Loans accrues at the rate of inflation (Retail Price Index) plus 3% while a student is at university and up until the April after they finish their studies for those living in England and Wales. Those living in Scotland and Northern Ireland pay a flat rate of 0.9% (2015/16 rate), although this is subject to annual review. Thereafter, interest costs may reduce dependent on income. Currently, those living in England and Wales pay interest at RPI if their income is £21,000 or less rising on a sliding scale up to RPI plus 3% where income is £41,000 or above, whilst those from Scotland and Northern Ireland pay a flat rate of 0.9%. ■

moodboard/THINKSTOCK

AUTHOR'
TIPS

6 THINGS YOU'LL NEED FOR THE APPLICATION

1 **Proof of identity,** e.g. passport or birth certificate.

2 **Bank account details.** This must be a UK bank account in your son or daughter's name.

3 **National Insurance number.** Your child will have been sent this number shortly before their 16th birthday.

4 **Proposed course and university** (this information can be amended at a later date).

5 **Household income** (earned and unearned).

6 Details of any **dependent children**.

Parenting

Creatas Images/THINKSTOCK

Parents may feel excluded from the university application process; it can seem as though their child and the school are 'just getting on with it'. How can you help them make a wise choice without seeming to take over? Some teenagers are happy to engage in reasoned discussion and genuinely value the experience and input their parents offer; others will bristle at any hint of parental interference. Resolving disagreements requires high level diplomacy skills. However strongly you feel, first and foremost you must be prepared to listen. After that, the ability to make positive suggestions calmly and a genuine willingness to compromise will also help. Bear in mind that your child could in theory submit their application without consulting you at all.

ASK YOURSELF...

Am I projecting my own ideas/ambitions/concerns onto my child's decision? If you have strong feelings about a particular aspect of university life, consider whether these may stem from something in your own history. This will help you focus on your child's best interests, not your own.

TREAD CAREFULLY

Typical flashpoints are choice of subject and university, but commenting on their lack of urgency with regard to research, booking open days or writing the Personal Statement can also produce aggravation.

LEARN TOGETHER

Don't assume you know the ropes; things have changed since you were at school/university. Familiarise yourself with the UCAS process, that way you can ask the right questions at the right time.

Many schools host UCAS information evenings featuring presentations from university admissions staff. Find out about them in advance and arrange to accompany your child.

ASK YOURSELF...

Am I worried about how the family dynamic will change when my child goes to university?

ASK YOUR CHILD...

What advice has the school given you?

IS HIGHER EDUCATION THE RIGHT PATH?

Going to university is now the default option after A levels, but is higher education the right path for everyone?

Choosing whether to apply to university is likely to be one of the most important decisions your child has had to make so far. Conflicting stories in the media about the benefits (or otherwise) that may be conferred by a university education can often generate much confusion for both parents and students. It's worth noting that university isn't just about academic study. Many successful actors, journalists, musicians and sportspeople found their niche while at university. Student politics or debating societies have also been the proving ground for many of our leading statesmen and women. Where to study, what to study and how much it will cost all need to be considered and no viable option should be off the table—at least to start with.

Professional necessity

For vocational careers such as medicine, dentistry, veterinary medicine, law, teaching, nursing and midwifery, a degree is a requirement to enter the profession. An increasing number of other jobs now also stipulate a degree as an entry level must-have. This being the case, a degree will open up many more career opportunities for your son or daughter. Without a degree they will, for instance, be excluding themselves from the prospect of securing a place on the growing number of graduate schemes, which most of the top UK companies offer, and which come with very attractive salaries and excellent career progression.

Learning and earning

There is a significant potential economic benefit to having a degree. Recent Office of National Statistics Labour Market research (2012) highlights some key advantages of being a graduate, including lower unemployment rates and higher earnings. A January 2012 report by investment firm Skandia concludes that gaining a degree is the best option for young people today in terms of earnings potential. An average graduate is expected to earn £1.6 million over their working life, over 60% more than those with only A levels.

Recent studies conducted by High Fliers Research Limited, a leading independent market research company specialising in graduate recruitment, provide further evidence of a positive outlook for graduates. The number of graduates recruited by companies within the Times Top 100 Graduate Employers increased by 3.3% in 2015 and these firms plan to expand their graduate recruitment level by a further 7.5% in 2016. In addition, graduate starting salaries are projected to remain unchanged in 2016 at an average of £30,000 per annum.

All the evidence points to a degree as a significant economic advantage. ▶

According to UCAS, 532,000 people applied to university in 2015, an increase of 3.1% on the previous year and the highest number so far recorded.

Top graduate salaries start with the investment banks (£47,000 average), legal firms (£41,000 average) and banking and finance companies (£36,000 average). Among some of the highest in 2015 were Aldi (£42,000) and the European Commission (£41,500).

High Fliers – The Graduate Market in 2016

IN THE KNOW

The Confederation of British Industry (CBI) defines employability skills as follows:

- **A positive attitude:** readiness to take part, openness to new ideas and activities, desire to achieve
- **Self-management:** readiness to accept responsibility, flexibility, time management, readiness to improve own performance
- **Team working:** respecting others, co-operating, negotiating/persuading, contributing to discussions
- **Business and customer awareness:** basic understanding of the key drivers for business success and the need to provide customer satisfaction
- **Problem solving:** analysing facts and circumstances and applying creative thinking to develop appropriate solutions
- **Communication and literacy:** application of literacy, ability to produce clear, structured written work and oral literacy, including listening and questioning
- **Application of numeracy:** manipulation of numbers, general mathematical awareness and its application in practical contexts
- **Application of Information Technology:** basic IT skills, including familiarity with word processing, spreadsheets, file management and use of Internet search engines.

CBI – 'Future fit: Preparing graduates for the world of work' 2009

Wavebreak Media/THINKSTOCK

THE INSIDE TRACK

"Compared to school leavers, university graduates have more experience of life and have a tendency to have thought harder about, and planned more carefully, their career path. The disciplines of their education make them ready for the rigours of paid work.

However, school leavers tend to be more malleable and easier to train. They can be keener to prove themselves but have lower (and often more realistic) expectations.

School leavers rarely think they should be running meetings within a year of starting a new job; it is often quite surprising how quickly university graduates think they should be trusted with judgements that they are often incapable of making."

SENIOR MANAGER IN A LEADING FINANCIAL INSTITUTION

Academic challenge

University gives students the opportunity to study a subject they enjoy in real depth. It can also offer them the chance to pursue a new subject, perhaps one they haven't studied formally at school but in which they have developed an interest. Either way it's important to choose a degree course carefully; remember, being good at a subject is not always the same as being interested in it. Unlike school, at university no-one will be standing over students to ensure they attend lectures or complete assignments. Without a genuine commitment to their subject, your child will have little motivation to stay the course.

Experience

While this is all valuable, we must not lose sight of the fact that many people cite their time at university as the happiest years of their lives. There will be the opportunity to meet new people from all over the world, to develop independence by living alone and to broaden horizons. Even if your child's career doesn't require a degree, they may benefit from university in a multitude of other ways. ■

"As the mother of twins, one not so academically minded, the other bright, we had a real dilemma when it came to deciding on university or not. But in the end, listening to our children, it became very clear one just would not cope and quite frankly would not manage the work load expected at university. That child is now earning a good wage in London, having got there through hard work, charm and confidence. He has an unstinting belief in himself as he didn't go to university and fail. The other twin is loving university but already has debt, and can see many benefits in gaining a career from a different pathway."

KATE, MOTHER OF 19-YEAR-OLD TWINS

IS IT BETTER TO APPLY BEFORE OR AFTER EXAM RESULTS?

Most students apply to university before they have completed their final exams and, if they are successful, will generally be offered a place conditional on results. Typically for a Russell Group university, this will be around three As at A level or 36 points at IB, but offers vary between institutions and subjects. Some universities (for example Birmingham, Lancaster, Nottingham) are now offering some unconditional places, but this is still quite unusual. Others stipulate A*s in the offer (usually for a very oversubscribed course) or specify a minimum grade in a specific subject.

UCAS has systems to deal quickly with results which are different from those predicted or expected. UCAS Clearing (see p. 87) can help with those who have underperformed, while those applicants who have done better than anticipated can often gain a place at a university which might have initially rejected them through the underused UCAS Adjustment process (see p. 90).

Students considering a gap year (**see p. 22**) before starting university may decide to apply after they have left school or, if they are not happy with the offers they received first time round, to withdraw their initial application and reapply the following year. ▶

THE INSIDE TRACK

"Although most of our applicants have still to sit their final school examinations, we welcome applications from those who have already taken their A levels or other final school examinations. We try to judge these applicants on the same basis as those who have still to complete their school careers, whilst making allowance for the extra year's experience and maturity such applicants should have. We expect applicants in this category to have achieved at least A*AA at A2 level (or equivalent)."

CLARE COLLEGE, CAMBRIDGE

Students at Cranleigh are jubilant after receiving their A Level results

THE INSIDE TRACK

"Competition for places is extremely high and applicants who apply during their year out with qualifications achieved may be in a stronger position than those who apply for deferred entry with predicted grades."
EDINBURGH UNIVERSITY

5 **ADVANTAGES** OF POST-QUALIFICATION APPLICATIONS

1 Your child will know what their grades are and therefore the courses for which they are qualified.

2 **They have more time and evidence to decide what they want to study; a post-qualification application (PQA) is good for someone who is genuinely uncertain about their course or university choices.**

3 They have more time to prepare for specialist tests and interviews; of particular benefit to an Oxbridge candidate.

4 It is easier to write a Personal Statement (or school reference) if there is evidence of exam performance. An extra year also gives more to write about.

5 They have the opportunity for more extensive work experience and wider reading to support their application.

As far as universities are concerned, they simply want to attract the best students and do not mind whether these are applying before or after qualifications. However, there is a debate as to whether all applications should be post-qualification, particularly because predicted grades are not that accurate. With the demise of the AS exam, widely regarded by universities as a fairly reliable indicator of A2 performance, universities are even more dependent on the schools' predicted grades. The debate over shifting application for all to the post-qualification period is likely to continue.

Playing the system

Demographic changes (such as a particularly high or low annual birth rate) and alterations in university funding can affect the numbers applying in any given year. For example, gap year numbers plummeted in 2011, the year before the government's changes to tuition fees, as students took up places in advance of the fee increase. This meant university applications were slightly down in 2012.

It's hard to plan for this kind of thing, as it only applies if such a change coincides with your child's final years at school. Nevertheless such factors could play a part in deciding the year in which to submit an application, especially for a borderline candidate. UCAS produces its own application statistics, but these should be used with caution: your child's application should be determined by aptitude and ambition rather than the statistical possibilities involved.

Which is easier?

On balance, it is probably easier to apply while still at school where there will be advice and support constantly available. Despite the best intentions of your child and their former school, it is not always easy to deal with the practicalities of application quickly, efficiently and with personalised, individual attention if they are no longer at school on a regular basis. On the other hand, universities may be more easily persuaded by hard evidence of exam results on which to decide about an offer. ■

POST-APPLICATION

"As I post-applied there has definitely been less of a stressful waiting experience compared to last year, as you already know your set grades and so have a better idea of what universities' responses may be."

Katie, applicant for Politics & International Relations

Pupil and mistress at Oakham School

AUTHOR'S TIPS

4 DISADVANTAGES OF POST-QUALIFICATION APPLICATIONS

1 **Your child will be detached from the school advice and support network and, while schools should continue to provide guidance, this may not always be practical to access.**

2 The practicalities of application may interfere with your child's gap year activities: Oxbridge interviews in December, for example, can cut across plans and cannot be rescheduled.

3 Your child may lose some of their academic edge, motivation and enthusiasm.

4 **Your child will be competing against applicants reapplying after an unsuccessful first attempt, who will have learned more about the application process.**

TO GAP OR NOT TO GAP?

Some students can't wait to start at university; others want to step off the academic express and do something completely different before starting their degree.

Students take a gap year between school and university for many reasons. For some it is a chance to travel or to pursue other interests; others use the time to resit exams, take part in work experience projects or earn money. Postponing a gap year until after graduation or even taking one between jobs is now becoming more common.

Most universities support the idea of a gap year and respond positively to applicants who have made imaginative, relevant and constructive plans. Your child should explain in their Personal Statement how their plans are relevant to their chosen course of study. However, they are equally clear that, valuable as the experience can be, it is in no way essential—and there may be disadvantages for some areas of study. Anyone considering a gap year should look carefully at the policy of the university and department to which they are applying. It is also advisable to contact the university to confirm their position on gap years.

The number of UCAS applicants taking gap years varies between around 7–10%.

Deferred entry

Some university departments are reluctant to defer places for students wanting a gap year, believing that it results in a deterioration in academic skills.

While Oxford and Cambridge are in general sympathetic to applicants who want to take a gap year, they are sometimes unwilling to tie up places for the following year, when the overall standard of candidates might be higher. It is therefore quite possible that if your child has applied to Oxbridge and indicated in their Personal Statement that they would like a gap year, they will be offered a place only on condition that they do not take a year out. If your child decides they want a gap year after already receiving an offer for the coming September, ▶

Gap years involving travel abroad can typically cost between £4,000 and £10,000 (plus provision for contingencies).

Monkeybusinessimages/iStock/THINKSTOCK

AUTHOR'S TIPS

PROS & CONS OF TAKING A GAP YEAR

PRO: It's a chance to earn money and gain work experience.

PRO: You can volunteer for charitable and environmental projects abroad.

PRO: A break from education is a chance to find out more about yourself.

PRO: On a gap year you broaden your knowledge of the world and meet new people.

PRO: A year out working or travelling may bring greater confidence and maturity.

CON: Are these experiences really going to be that different from a first year at university?

CON: Gap year travel can be very expensive; is it worth it?

CON: You might be having fun but are you sure you're really making a difference?

CON: Or maybe you're just procrastinating!

CON: It's a well trodden path; are you really learning anything new?

THE INSIDE TRACK

"I took a gap year myself before coming to university and I'd recommend the experience to anybody, whether you know what you want to do after university or not. I took a gap year in Kenya, working as a volunteer in a luxury tented camp teaching water skiing for six months, which was quite a unique experience. I had an amazing experience while I was out there and I think it really aided me both getting into university in the first place and applying for graduate jobs afterwards. My gap year taught me skills of independence and self-reliance that I was able to use at university and in life afterwards. You can tell in the first week of university who's taken a gap year and who hasn't; it tends to be those who come forward and are more socially active that have had a bit more life experience, and also those who are a bit more outspoken on their course. The lecturers love that.

AN ACADEMIC AT BIRMINGHAM UNIVERSITY

Everste/iStock/THINKSTOCK

the university may be sympathetic but is not obliged to defer the offer. Your teenager will need to consider their priorities carefully in these situations; they may not get the same offer the following year.

If your son or daughter is already set on taking a gap year, then they can of course apply through UCAS after they have left school. **(See more on post-qualification applications on p. 19.)**

A year out as part of your degree

Some university courses allow students the option of spending a year away from the university, often with the chance of working abroad. What used to be the preserve of Modern Linguists and a few students on exchange or international programmes is now available to many more: the University of Bath, for example, has a work placement scheme available to students on all courses, with voluntary and paid placements. Such arrangements will involve an extra year of study; the placement (or year out) will usually be between the second and third years of a normal degree course.

The cost

For some students, gap years are a chance to work and earn money to help support themselves at university. If they continue to live at home, then clearly the costs are minimal and the financial benefits can be considerable. It is also possible for the gap experience abroad to include paid employment (eg TEFL teaching; sports coaching; working as a ski-chalet host) and thereby become self-financing, at least in terms of living costs. ■

THE INSIDE TRACK

"Making a successful application for deferred entry is seen as slightly more competitive since the college is effectively committing to a decision on your application before they have seen other students applying in the following year."

OXFORD UNIVERSITY

WHAT MAKES A USEFUL GAP YEAR?

A gap year may seem like a great idea, but your child needs to be sure they'll make the most of the experience.

melis82/iStock/THINKSTOCK

There is no such thing as the 'right' gap year: finding the right fit for the individual student is what will make the difference. Ideally a gap year should include activities that will enable your child to grow in new directions and be better able to embark on their degree course and subsequent career.

Most students pursue more than one activity during their gap year, typically spending half of it earning money and then going abroad, either to work, to travel, to learn a language or to participate in, for example, a conservation project. Other gap year activities include internships, pursuing further study or taking courses in practical skills such as cookery or car maintenance.

The gap year is now a thriving industry with over 300 companies offering projects ranging from working with wild animals in Bolivia to joining the crew of a tall ship. Many capitalise on the idealism of youth, promoting environmental and social causes with the additional lure of 'adrenaline pumping' activities such as white water rafting.

These projects may be good for the participants, but it can be hard to gauge objectively what benefits reach the causes they claim to serve. If this is a worry then it's worth researching smaller scale companies with a direct ▶

IN THE KNOW

"A work placement—particularly one that is relevant to a career—will add value to CVs, helping young people to stand out from the crowd in the job market."

CALLUM KENNEDY, DIRECTOR OF BUNAC VOLUNTEER PROGRAMMES

TAKEN FROM A 2012 DAILY TELEGRAPH ARTICLE

Wavebreakmedia Ltd/THINKSTOCK

Vingeran/iStock/THINKSTOCK

link to less glamorous local charity projects in countries like India.

The choice of what to do is enormous, and there is something to fit every type of personality and outlook.

Logistics

If your child is resitting exams or applying to university during the year, then activities need to be arranged around the exam and application timetables. This is particularly important for Oxbridge applications: Oxford and Cambridge colleges will not reschedule December interviews to fit in with your child's gap year plans, and there are often demanding tests and time-consuming work to submit beforehand. ■

THE INSIDE TRACK

"Research shows that students who take a well-planned, structured year out are more likely to be satisfied with their choice of course and, even better, more likely to complete it.

You should include your plans for a gap year in your UCAS form Personal Statement. You will need to outline how you plan to spend the time and what you hope to gain from it (a suntan doesn't count). We're happy to talk to students about their plans and hear what they intend to do during their "year off".

Admissions tutors are looking for coherence and a clear plan from the applicant's statement. If you don't know what you are going to do, then you will have a hard time convincing anyone else how worthwhile your gap year will be."

QUEEN MARY UNIVERSITY OF LONDON

THE INSIDE TRACK

"Where mathematics is important for your course, it would be wise to take steps to ensure that your maths does not get rusty during your year out. Many students take a further qualification in maths (A level Further Mathematics, STEP etc) or make good use of resources such as NRICH. Keeping languages going is also important for some subjects. In all cases (whether you are studying, working or volunteering) we hope that you will continue to develop your academic interests during your gap year."

KING'S COLLEGE, CAMBRIDGE

Strahidimitrov/iStock/THINKSTOCK

Parenting

Through this period of decision making, your child may be receiving very little guidance or conversely an abundance of advice from a variety of sources, much of which may be conflicting. You can help them to consider and evaluate the pros and cons of university and gap years, and which is the most appropriate path for your child to take.

Young people can feel pressured into making particular choices by the expectations of their parents, either real or perceived, or by the behaviour of their peers. The more open-minded and encouraging you can be in discussing your child's post-school options, the higher the chance they will make a wise choice.

cwa-studios/iStock/THINKSTOCK

ASK YOUR CHILD...

- Do you really want to go to university?
- What do you think is the point of going to university?
- If you didn't go to university, what might you do instead?

ASK YOURSELF...

Why do (or don't) I want my child to go to university, or to take a gap year?

Will I find it hard to let go?

BE FRANK

When making decisions with your son or daughter, openly discuss the negative aspects of each decision: they may not have thought of the downside. In discussing what could go wrong, you might ask them 'How would you cope if that happened?' This gives your child the chance to express their own apprehensions.

MONEY TALKS

Talk about finance, particularly if you are not in a position to provide financial support or are unwilling to do so. You don't want to make your child feel guilty about spending money on themselves, but they need to take financial responsibility for any decisions they make.

THINGS YOUR CHILD MIGHT WORRY ABOUT

- Am I really good enough for university?
- Will I be out of my depth socially?
- How will I deal with the day-to-day practicalities of life away from home?
- Do I want the pressure of having to get high grades hanging over me?
- Will I miss my home, family, friends, pets?
- How will going away affect my relationships?
- Will I end up with a huge debt to repay?

HOW IMPORTANT IS CHOOSING THE RIGHT SUBJECT?

Choosing your course is arguably more important than choosing your university; in fact it may be the most critical part of the whole application.

Ideally your child should start the application process by choosing the subject or subjects they want to study—or at least narrowing down the field to a general area such as politics, business or international relations. There are those who put their choice of university first—'I am desperate to go to Oxford and don't mind what I study'—but the university will quickly see through the lack of commitment to a particular discipline.

It's important to remember that the level of the offer or grade requirement is not necessarily an indication of the quality of the course; it is the result of demand and popularity (which may indicate quality, but not always). ■

AUTHOR'S TIPS

10 TIPS FOR CHOOSING A COURSE

1. Your child should **research thoroughly** and stay open-minded.
2. **Don't be influenced** by other people's choice of course or university.
3. All your child's UCAS choices should be for the **same or similar subjects;** they can only write one Personal Statement.
4. They should definitely **study a subject they enjoy;** three or four years is a long time to spend doing something they dislike.
5. Selecting one or more of their A level or IB Higher subjects as a degree course is a popular option—but your child should **look at related subjects as well,** particularly if they are less well known.
6. **Combined and joint courses** are a chance to follow more than one interest; this broader education may be attractive to employers.
7. Read the small print. If your child's predicted exam grades do not match the **course requirements,** they are likely to be rejected.
8. Make sure any other **entry requirements** (specialist tests, GCSE grades etc) are being met.
9. Your child doesn't have to match their course to the **job** they want to do; very few BBC employees are media studies graduates.
10. Check out **graduate employment statistics,** especially if your child has a particular career in mind.

Purestock/THINKSTOCK

DOES THE CHOICE OF COURSE AFFECT CAREER PROSPECTS?

Depending on the career your child has in mind, their choice of subject may not be entirely relevant.

A university education is partly a preparation for the world of work and, with this in mind, it is tempting to see the choice of subject in narrowly utilitarian or vocational terms. There are professions which require the study of a specific subject at university—medicine, engineering and architecture are obvious examples—and if your child is absolutely certain about their career path, then a vocational course may be the right choice. Moreover, these fields are broad and varied enough to accommodate several changes of direction. However, at a time when we are told that young people today can expect to make four or five major changes of direction during their professional lives, will a narrowly vocational degree course be flexible enough? Does a degree in librarianship or physiotherapy necessarily put you in a position to adapt to such changes?

In favour of non-vocational courses

Many lawyers, bankers and business leaders initially studied subjects which were not directly relevant to law, finance or management, acquiring their professional expertise through postgraduate qualifications or on-the-job training and experience. Employers often value the intellectual breadth of someone who has not pursued a vocational course: many subjects will enable your child to develop the all-important transferable skills which can be applied to a whole range of careers while allowing them to push to the limit their enthusiasm for a subject they love. People who can think with originality, ▶

The only careers for which a vocational first degree is virtually mandatory are medicine, dentistry and veterinary science, though even here there are those who might begin with a course in biomedical science or animal science and then move on to medicine or veterinary science.

Most engineers study the subject at university—though a degree in science or maths might allow someone to move into engineering. Architecture similarly usually requires a specialist first degree.

A STUDENT SPEAKS

VOCATIONAL COURSES

"My degree in journalism was certainly an excellent preparation for my career in the profession. However, the breadth of associated disciplines covered throughout my three years of university study (which included public relations, marketing and communications) has supported my career change into Public Relations and, most recently, Marketing. Indeed, when I was considering a move from journalism, I felt that my degree course had given me a variety of excellent transferable skills that would make me a competitive applicant for a wide range of professions. I don't believe my degree course limited me in any way and, in fact, it also provided me with a competitive edge in a range of professions."

Ian, Journalism Graduate from Bournemouth University

THE INSIDE TRACK

"Unless an employer has defined their needs very narrowly in terms of a vocational degree, the choice of subject is less critical than the quality of degree and university. That said, the most important thing of all is how candidates can explain how that degree had helped them develop as people and equipped them to tackle the next set of challenges."

SIR IAN CHESHIRE, CHAIRMAN OF DEBENHAMS

individuality and scepticism are always in demand—hence the enduring popularity of humanities degrees.

If your child wants to be an aeronautical engineer, a general engineering undergraduate course may be the best route, with specialisation further down the line. If they want to be an arts or sports administrator, then a general course in business and management could suit them and teach a broader range of skills. Careers such as journalism or TV production can be explored by students of, say, History or English, through editing the university newspaper or running the campus TV service, rather than by following a specialist course.

A degree in Law has obvious attractions for those aspiring to be lawyers—but there are plenty of ways to qualify in the subject after a first degree in another discipline.

In favour of vocational courses

If your child has a specific career in mind, then the choice of a vocational course may be determined by whether they want to enter that career straight from university with the relevant degree, say in accountancy, sports management or actuarial science, or spend some more time getting experience and qualifications afterwards. In the present competitive economic environment it may be that both you and your child feel it is best for them to get into the job market at the earliest opportunity—and a vocational course may therefore be the best route for them.

Joint courses can give the best of both worlds, where career training can be combined with a more purely cerebral subject. Even with vocational subjects it may be better to study a more general undergraduate course and specialise at postgraduate level. ■

THE INSIDE TRACK

"I believe in education producing all-rounders. Study what you are passionate about, and a future as a lawyer, accountant, marketing executive, interior designer etc can still be yours."

SENIOR MANAGER IN A UK-BASED FINANCIAL INSTITUTION

IS SCHOOL EXAM PERFORMANCE A GOOD BASIS FOR DEGREE CHOICE?

Children often excel at what they enjoy the most, but is the subject they find easy at school one that will keep them interested for three years or more at university?

Fourth Form boy at Cranleigh School

Jetta Productions/DIGITALVISION/THINKSTOCK

If your child applies for a course in a subject they are studying at school, universities will certainly look closely at their exam results in that subject. If the results are less than impressive they will expect to see at least evidence of aptitude for further study. This is where the school's reference can be of particular importance. There are, of course, differences between school and university approaches to a subject, but an A level or IB course is still seen as an excellent foundation for studying that subject at university. Some universities will also look closely at your child's GCSE profile.

For most students, success and enjoyment go together: they have no problem in focusing time and effort on a subject they love, though, even here, they may need encouragement to divert their attention towards those aspects which they find less attractive. To study a subject for three or more years requires real commitment, and ideally your child should love the subject for which they are applying—or at least be prepared to work hard for the length of the course because they feel the rewards at the end will be worth the effort.

Economics requires a high level of mathematical ability and grade A or A* in Maths at A level is a grade requirement at most Russell Group universities. A top grade in Economics A level is not enough on its own.

If there are real problems in getting good exam results in a subject which your child loves and is really determined to study, then you need to talk with the school: there may be extenuating circumstances or the university course may be so different from the subject syllabus at school as to make the exam performance irrelevant. The school will also be aware of the grades which different universities will require and guide your child in a direction where they are more likely to get realistic offers. Further, the school reference or direct contact with the university may be able to deal with the issues.

In the end, however, this may be the time to be realistic about overly-optimistic ambitions and accept that never will my child be a fully-fledged vet—but what about those courses in animal zoology or equine studies? There will always be an alternative route and accepting disappointment at this stage may open up other opportunities.

Things to look out for

Caution is advised if your child is selecting a university course solely on the basis that it is their best examination subject at school; the degree course may be radically different in its content and demands from the subject at sixth form level. As in so many aspects of the application process, the only way round this dilemma is rigorous research so that your child knows exactly what will be expected of them.

It may be that your child intends to apply for a subject which they have not chosen to study in the sixth form—or which may not even be taught at their school. In some cases, this is not a problem: economics departments often prefer a good maths result to A level Economics; if you want to study Politics, then History is still seen as providing the right sort of foundation. In their Personal Statement, your child might mention that they deliberately chose an A level programme excluding the subject they intended following at university to gain a broader range of relevant skills. However, it is important to look closely at the entrance requirement for courses in a particular subject—and these vary between universities: there can often be requirements for a sixth form qualification in particular subjects, particularly for sciences. ■

THE INSIDE TRACK

"It's important to have, and to cultivate, a solid interest in the subject. Students should be empowered to pursue their individual passions not only in addition to their academic studies, but within their studies too. It is usually this combination which leads to the best results, as well as the most interesting careers!"

MARIANNA KOLI, NEW COLLEGE OF THE HUMANITIES

SHOULD THE POPULARITY OF A DEGREE COURSE INFLUENCE YOUR CHILD'S CHOICE?

'There are lies, damned lies and statistics'—and anyone would be unwise to play the numbers game and base a university application solely on abstract statistics.

UCAS provides a wealth of statistical information after the close of business each year, but it requires skill and scepticism to use it productively to help choose a subject to study at university. Individual universities are more guarded about publishing rates of acceptance, partly because they do not want to put off applicants. It is also important to remember that statistics do not give you the whole picture. Statistically it can look easier to get into a university studying Classics than other subjects because there are fewer students studying the subject and therefore fewer applications, and in some disciplines statistically it is easier to get a place at Oxford compared to some other universities. This does not take into account the standards required for particular courses that have nothing to do with how many people apply.

The popularity of a subject needs to be seen in relation to the number of places available—statistically, the hardest subject for which to get a place ▶

Pupils at Cranleigh School

is probably Veterinary Medicine simply because so few universities teach it and it is extremely popular, attracting vast numbers of well-qualified applicants. On the other hand, while getting a place to study History at Durham or Bristol may be highly competitive, there are plenty of other options, particularly if your child considers related subjects or joint courses.

If your child is keen to study a popular subject and their school thinks this is realistic, then encourage them to go ahead. What is important is to make sure that they will meet the predicted grade requirements for the course they want to pursue: failure to do so will be a wasted choice. In addition you should encourage them to look at universities which might initially not be in their sights—overcoming the bane of the 'fashionable', 'acceptable' or 'parents'-choice' university list—and the broader or joint courses encompassing their chosen subject. In the end, almost all UCAS applicants will gain a place somewhere in the higher education system, though flexibility and adaptability helps. ■

According to UCAS, in January 2015 the most popular courses were:

- Subjects allied to medicine—includes biochemistry and physiotherapy but not medicine itself (358,040 entrants)
- Business and Admin studies (300,070)
- Biological Sciences (258,410)
- Creative Arts and Design—graphic design, illustration, textiles, fashion, interior design, animation etc (247,290)
- Social Studies—includes economics, geography, anthropology, criminology, psychology, social work (220,000)
- Engineering (151,840)
- Law (118,630)
- Computer Science (113,730)
- Physical Sciences—includes chemistry, physics, geology (102,950)
- Medicine and Dentistry (86,650)
- Education (82,240)
- History and Philosophical Studies (79,540)
- Linguistics, Classics and Related Subjects—includes English (61,070)
- Mass Communications and Documentation (58,410)
- Sciences combined with social sciences or arts (54,140)

HERE TO HELP

"The more competitive the course, the more essential it is for students to select a range of universities to ensure they secure some offers. A good test is if they would rather do their chosen subject at their "fifth choice" than a different subject at a university they prefer."

MARY BREEN, HE ADMISTRESS OF ST MARY'S SCHOOL ASCOT

Parenting

We like to think that as parents we always put our child's interests first, but when it comes to their academic interests we may not be the best judges. Children often acquire fixed roles in families very early on—the sporty one, the bookish one, the arty one etc—and it can be hard, especially for parents, to see beyond these long after they've ceased to be accurate. You may not be aware of having applied any pressure on your child to choose a certain subject, but that doesn't mean a young person won't feel the weight of expectation.

Fuse/THINKSTOCK

REMIND YOURSELF

It is your child who will be spending three years or more studying a subject at university and it's crucial that the subject is their choice and not one they're doing because parents want them to.

MAKE COMPROMISES

You want your child to study Accountancy; they want Drama. Perhaps there's a Theatre Studies and Management course which will satisfy both sides.

Talking with the school can help too. Schools are good at resolving conflict and will usually be honest about the rights and wrongs of a situation, even though they may often use their knowledge of your child to advise you to go with what your child wants.

ASK YOUR CHILD...

Why do you want to go to university to study this subject? Prompts might include: Enjoyment? Good at it? Status and future income? Everyone else is doing so? Get away from home? Be independent and grow up? Social life?

Getting them to 'sell' you their decision can often be revealing—on both sides.

IF YOU DON'T AGREE...

Try asking:

- **Have you thought about other subjects you might like to study?**
- **What is it that interests you about the subject you have chosen?**
- **What advice have you received from your teachers?**
- **Why do you think we (parents) might have reservations about your choice?**

ASK YOURSELF...

Am I basing my judgement of a subject on the reputation it had when I was at school? Things change. Geography, for example, was once seen as an 'easy' option but today it is a highly respected degree course with myriad applications in the world of work.

WHAT DIFFERENCE DOES CHOOSING THE RIGHT UNIVERSITY MAKE?

The best university for your child will prepare them effectively for the rest of their life.

We all think we know a 'good' university when we see it, but the criteria for judging any educational institution are varied and complex. The vast majority do a really good job for their students, and most students are reasonably happy with the education they receive according to surveys of student satisfaction.

Teaching techniques

Most universities use a combination of teaching techniques: lectures, seminars, classes and small group or one-to-one tutorials (this latter largely the preserve of Oxbridge or smaller independent institutions such as the University of Buckingham or the New College of the Humanities). Scientists will have plenty of laboratory work and many universities provide opportunities for practical experience, work placements and study abroad.

See if you can find the 'contact hours' for your child's course on the university website. Contact hours are the amount of timetabled teaching—whether lectures, seminars or tutorials—and

AUTHOR'S TIPS

10 THINGS TO CONSIDER WHEN **CHOOSING A UNIVERSITY**

1 How **competitive** would your child want the academic environment to be? The competition for places may reflect this.

2 Does it teach the **subject** or subject combination your child wants—and does it do it well?

3 Will your child be in a strong position to **get a job** at the end of the course?

4 Is the **system of teaching** right for your child? Is the exam and assessment system one which plays to your child's strengths?

5 Many courses, particularly the humanities and social sciences, will have **optional units**. Are there good choices on offer?

6 Does the university have the facilities for your child to follow their **non-academic interests?**

7 What are the **facilities** like for your child's chosen subject? This is especially important for sciences and subjects with a practical input. What is the library and ICT provision?

8 What will the **accommodation** be like? Will it involve lots of travelling? And how much will it cost?

9 How cosmopolitan is the **environment** of the university and its location? This may be important, for example, to applicants from an international background.

10 Does the university provide students on your child's course with opportunities for **work experience** and study abroad?

sborisov/iStock/THINKSTOCK

will differ according to subject. Students who need lots of feedback or who may find it hard to motivate themselves to study independently should think carefully about how they will manage their time.

Exams and assessment

If your child prefers coursework to formal examinations (or vice versa) then it's worth finding out about a university's assessment structure. The older universities still rely quite heavily on assessment through formal examinations and it is normal in a three-year course for there to be exams at the end of each year. Most courses involve an element of coursework ▶

> **Particular universities go in and out of fashion for all sorts of reasons, some of which have nothing to do with their academic reputation. Don't be surprised to hear places recommended solely for the quality of their night life!**

or a dissertation, while many universities now use more continuous methods of assessment for the final degree. For some young people continuous assessment can seem like a continuous examination and induce more stress over a longer period than a 'big bang' formal exam.

Prestige, reputation, specialism

Not all subjects are taught at all universities and the first line of research is to make sure that the subject your child wants to study is taught, and taught well, by their chosen institutions. Some universities are specialists with a reputation for excellence in specific areas—medical schools, LSE, Imperial College London, Courtauld Institute of Art, for example—though even these offer a broader range of courses than you might imagine.

Purestock/THINKSTOCK

Other universities have a reputation for excellence in certain areas—Law at Warwick, Economics at Bath, or History at York for example—but reputation is here, as elsewhere, anecdotal and subjective. Most universities teach most subjects well and it is more important that your child selects a university which will provide exactly the course they want rather than be swayed by hearsay and rumours about reputation.

It may be that your child is interested in a particular aspect of a subject—say South East Asian history, modern Indian literature or maritime engineering—and it is important that they apply for a course in which this interest can be explored; in this case, it is worth looking at lecturers' research interests and the options available within a course. ■

THE INSIDE TRACK

"We're blessed in the UK with a very strong and diverse university sector. Some of the differences are to do with day-to-day living preferences rather than anything academic. (Do they find collegiate universities supportive or claustrophobic? Are campus universities safe or cut off? Are cities lively or too noisy?) In terms of academic differences, some universities take a traditional and academic approach whereas others are focused on more vocationally-orientated skills. Getting the right match between university, subject, approach and student is important and students should research as widely as they can and visit a few universities to get a sense of what appeals to them."

SHEFFIELD UNIVERSITY

POST-APPLICATION

"The right course is the most crucial decision, as you actually have to study it for three or four years! But after picking the course, the choice of university is also an important factor. Think about whether you prefer larger cities or smaller cities, which each come with very different nightlife experiences. Look at the extracurricular activities on offer. Learn the difference between campus, city or collegiate universities. All these questions are central to your enjoyment of the university experience."

Izzy, History of Art student at Cambridge

WHERE CAN INFORMATION ON UNIVERSITIES BE FOUND?

There's no shortage of information about universities but not all of it is impartial or reliable. Attending an open day or arranging a visit is the best way to make your own decision.

While it is a good idea to attend open days or arrange visits to the top few universities which your child prefers, it is clearly impractical to visit all those which have courses, say in History, (probably well over 100) or even the top twenty of your child's shortlist. Schools are understandably reluctant to give students leave of absence during term to visit too many open days and a maximum of three or four visits is often imposed. Under the old AS/A2 system, there may have been more time after AS exams were completed to organise such visits: indeed, in some schools the main focus in the second half of the Year 12 summer term was on university application. However, with the adoption of linear, two-year A level courses in many schools, teaching will continue right to the end of the school year and your child cannot afford to miss too much school.

Before any visits are arranged or open days booked, your child should have undertaken their own extensive ▶

THIS MAY HELP

The Good Schools Guide has a wealth of information on universities, and offers a comprehensive Advice Service to pair your child up with the perfect university.

AUTHOR'S TIPS

7 PLACES **TO GET ADVICE**

1 **Former and present university students** will have an inside knowledge, and may even have insight into career prospects. Some universities will put you in touch with present or ex-students.

2 University **websites and prospectuses** are full of information—but remember that they are primarily marketing tools.

3 **Alternative university websites** are often set up by students and give a flavour of university life from a young person's perspective. (Watch out, though: it may be disgruntled students who make the effort to set up these sites, so the picture may be somewhat skewed.)

4 Students share their own experiences of the application system and the realities of undergraduate life on **student forums**.

5 University **open days**, visits and taster days provide a chance to ask awkward questions and discover if this really is where your child wants to be for three or four years.

6 Potential employers will have their own opinions on the best training for a particular career; it is not always the same as the opinion of school advisers and universities themselves.

7 **University League Tables** **(see p. 44)** are good if you are interested in the status of a university or a course—but don't let them put your child off applying for a course which seems right for them.

Hongqi Zang/iStock/THINKSTOCK

research, by looking at the UCAS website and the websites of the universities that attract them, and by talking to Careers counsellors and attending University Fairs.

Open days

Almost all universities hold open days. Your child will want to attend some of these themselves, but some universities offer specialised tours for parents as well, including presentations on key topics such as student finance, contact hours and accommodation.

Open days can be general or subject-specific but either way they should give your child the opportunity to see something of the university campus and gain an understanding of what life in the university is like. There will also be the opportunity to meet staff and current students—often doing the subject your child wants to study. Most open days provide specialist sessions for the main subject areas as part of a more general programme. There may even be a specimen lecture your child can attend.

Open days are marketing exercises and universities will obviously present themselves in the most positive light possible. It is therefore important that your child is prepared to ask probing questions and obtain satisfactory answers to any concerns they may have. Encourage them to be the one to ask the awkward question. If you are selling your house, then the person most likely to buy it is the one who asks the most demanding questions. It is the same with universities: the student who is really interested in going will want to

know everything about the place, warts and all.

If your child is attending an open day, try to make sure they also have time to explore the town or city in which the university is located—they need to know something about the environment beyond the university in which they will be living. This is particularly important if the university is on a campus or if student accommodation is located some distance from the main teaching site. ■

"Most of the information out there is aimed at students rather than parents. My daughters were given a lot of helpful advice—and had their own very strong opinions on where to apply. Instead of doing our own conflicting research, my wife and I spent our time listening and talking to our daughters. In the end, they knew best."

NICK, FATHER OF TWO GRADUATES

AUTHOR'S TIPS

11 QUESTIONS TO ASK AT AN OPEN DAY

1. What precise **work** are students expected to do? How will it be marked and assessed?
2. How much **contact time** is offered? How big are teaching groups?
3. What percentage of your students get Firsts and 2:1s?
4. What sort of **relationship** do your lecturers have with their students?
5. What sort of **jobs** do your graduates go on to?
6. What **support** is available if things go wrong? How many students drop out of this course each year?
7. What makes your course in this subject **different** from that at other universities?
8. Why is your university not in the top 20 (30 / 40 etc) of the **league tables**?
9. What are you looking for in a good **Personal Statement?**
10. How are **tuition fees** spent? Are they used to support the subject I will be studying?
11. How will my application be assessed?

We recommend...

THE GOOD SCHOOLS GUIDE

For nearly 30 years the Good Schools Guide has offered independent, unbiased and forthright advice from experts on all aspects of education. Whether you want to know about the primary school round the corner or applying to Harvard, our experts go beyond the prospectus and answer the questions that parents and students ask.

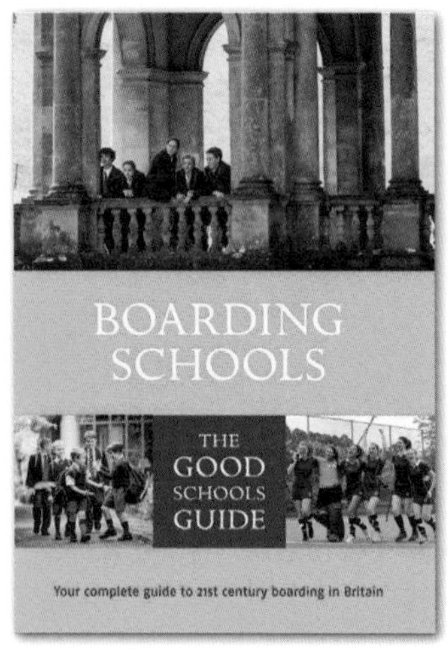

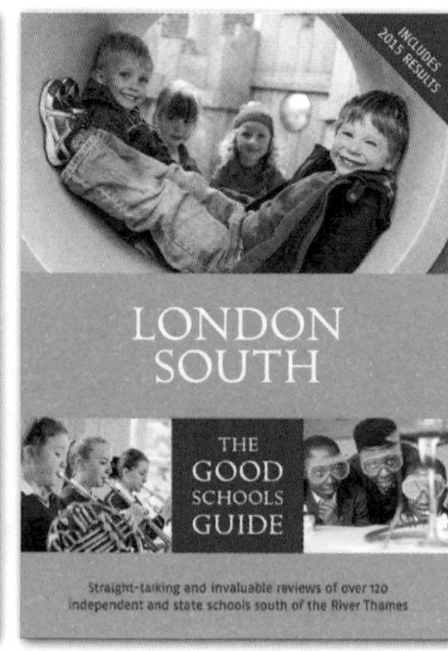

The Good Schools Guide online

Do you want to know how many pupils from a particular school regularly gain places at Oxford or Cambridge? Or the number who have gone on to study medicine over the last few years? With a subscription to the Good Schools Guide website you can customise your school search to your family's circumstances using their advanced search features.

As a subscriber you can read all the *Good Schools Guide*'s opinionated, detailed and informative reviews in full and can augment these by drawing on our unparalleled wealth of statistics and data, including most recent exam results. You will also have access to to hundreds of informative articles on all aspects of education, not to mention the *Good Schools Guide*'s popular blog. Subscriptions start at £15 for one month.

If you're looking for an international school for your child you'll want to subscribe to *The Good Schools Guide International*, which covers top international schools catering to English speaking expats in over 55 countries worldwide.

Get in touch: 0203 286 6824
www.goodschoolsguide.co.uk

University abroad?

Good Schools Guide expertise also extends to higher education. Our guide to US universities, *Uni in the USA and Beyond*, is the inside track on the hugely varied American higher education sector. Reviews are written by funny, sharp-eyed British students and cover not only the USA but also selected universities in Europe, China, Canada and Australia. *Uni in the USA and Beyond* is available as a paperback (£18) or online: www.uniintheusa.com

The Good Schools Guide Advice Service

You may have done your research, planned ahead and put your child's name down for a school in good time, but then the unexpected happens. It could be a new job, moving to a different country or discovering your child has dyslexia. If for any reason you find yourself having to start the school search again from scratch or under time pressure, let our experts help.

The Good Schools Guide Advice Service (GSGAS) is a personal service for families covering every aspect of schools and education. Our advisors are our most experienced and knowledgeable writers. They have visited countless schools, quizzed innumerable parents, childrne, teachers and head teachers. This vast experience, coupled with local knowledge, inside information and the shared expertise of the entire team, is available to GSGAS clients.

Because The Good Schools Guide Advice Service is a personal service, run on a one-to-one basis, we can help you in whatever way you need. You tell us what you want and we will tell you how we can help and work out a package to suit you. Our services range from a 30 minute telephone or Skype conversation to face to face advice, accompanied school visits, educational assessments and much, much more. We also offer:

- Expert advice on all aspects of SEN education
- A dedicated London service
- A scholarship and bursary service

Please see our website www.goodschoolsguide.co.uk/GSGAS http://www.gsgas.co.uk/ for full details.

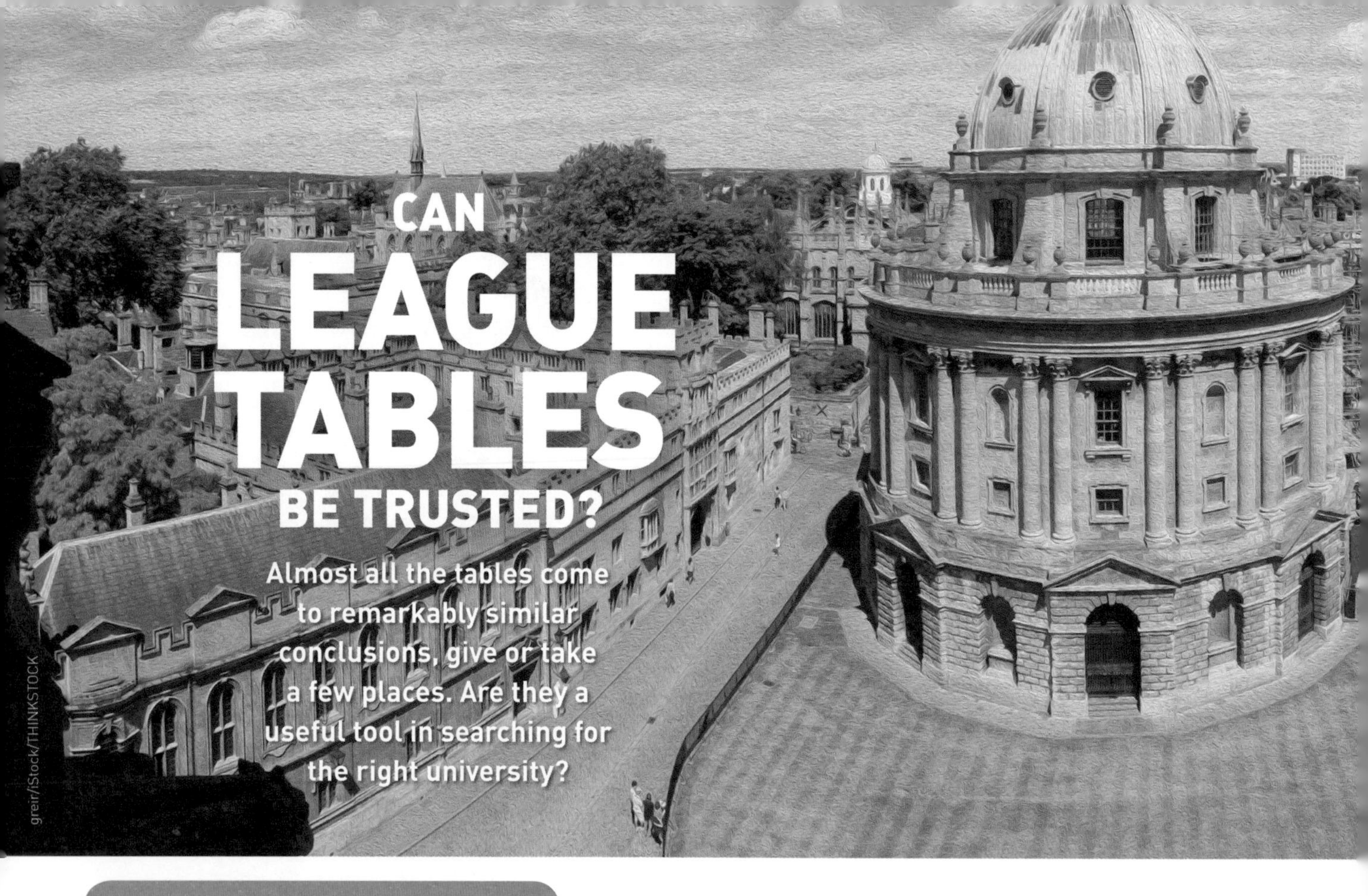

greir/iStock/THINKSTOCK

CAN LEAGUE TABLES BE TRUSTED?

Almost all the tables come to remarkably similar conclusions, give or take a few places. Are they a useful tool in searching for the right university?

THE COMPLETE UNIVERSITY GUIDE 2016 REFLECTS THE GENERAL TREND OF THE LEAGUE TABLES:

Ranking 2016	2015	
1	1	Cambridge
2	2	Oxford
3	3	LSE
4	6	Imperial College London
=5	5	Durham University
=5	4	St Andrews
7	7	Warwick
8	12	Surrey
9	11	Lancaster
10	9	UCL
11	10	Exeter
12	8	Bath
13	13	Loughborough
14	16	Southampton
15	18	Bristol
16	15	East Anglia
17	14	York
18	17	Birmingham
19	23	Leeds
20	21	Edinburgh

A number of commercial organisations and newspapers produce league tables to help in the choice of universities. These are based on extensive research and a complex system of awarding points for various factors such as student satisfaction, research assessment, graduate prospects, student/staff ratio and completion rates (how many students drop out).

Useful as these tables can be, it is difficult to know how rigorous the research has been, how effective the sampling is and whether the algorithms involved in producing the final statistics actually reflect what parents and students want to know.

In the end, what is important is that your child finds the course which is right for them and an academic and social atmosphere that is conducive to achieving success. They will increase the chance of reasonable offers by looking beyond the list of 'acceptable' or 'reputable' universities in the Russell Group and at the top of the league tables. Each individual is different—and there are universities to fit the needs of almost everyone who is suitable for a degree-level education.

Student satisfaction

The most useful aspect of the league tables is the breakdown of the figures—and the one perhaps to take notice of is that for 'student satisfaction'. While it is not always clear how students work out their satisfaction, this statistic is important if your child is to have a rewarding time at university. Other factors, such as

employment prospects, may interest you, but the academic performance of students may just reflect the ability of a university to attract high calibre applicants. If your child will thrive in an academically competitive atmosphere, it may be that a university high-up in the league tables will be right for them. However, much more important, is that the subject and course content are right for them—and it may be that they will actually cope better in a lower-ranked university.

Look at departments

It is crucial to look at individual courses, not just the universities as a whole. For example, Solent University may not be very high up the league table, but if you want to study Shipping and Port Management it is one of the best places in the world to do so.

Some universities publish more detailed statistics of performance by department—useful if you are keen to know how many Firsts and 2:1s are awarded which at least implies excellence in teaching. It can also be useful to know about the employment opportunities for graduates of a particular course. These statistics are not always easy to find on a website—don't be afraid to suggest that your child phones or emails a university to find out anything they need to know: they are, after all, the customer. The response of the university will say much about its attitude to potential applicants, which should reflect a concern to nurture and encourage the ambitions of each individual.

The Russell Group

24 of the top universities in the UK are represented by the Russell Group. On its website, the Russell Group describes its member universities as being 'committed to maintaining the very best research, [and] an outstanding teaching and learning experience'. Accurate enough—but the same description could be applied to many other institutions. Membership is largely confined to the older and red-brick universities. Some newer universities with a fine reputation, such as Bath, Sussex and East Anglia are not members. ■

RUSSELL GROUP UNIVERSITIES

- Birmingham
- Bristol
- Cambridge
- Cardiff
- Durham
- Edinburgh
- Exeter
- Glasgow
- Imperial College London
- King's College London
- Leeds
- Liverpool
- London School of Economics
- Manchester
- Newcastle
- Nottingham
- Oxford
- Queen Mary University of London
- Queen's Belfast
- Sheffield
- Southampton
- University College London
- Warwick
- York

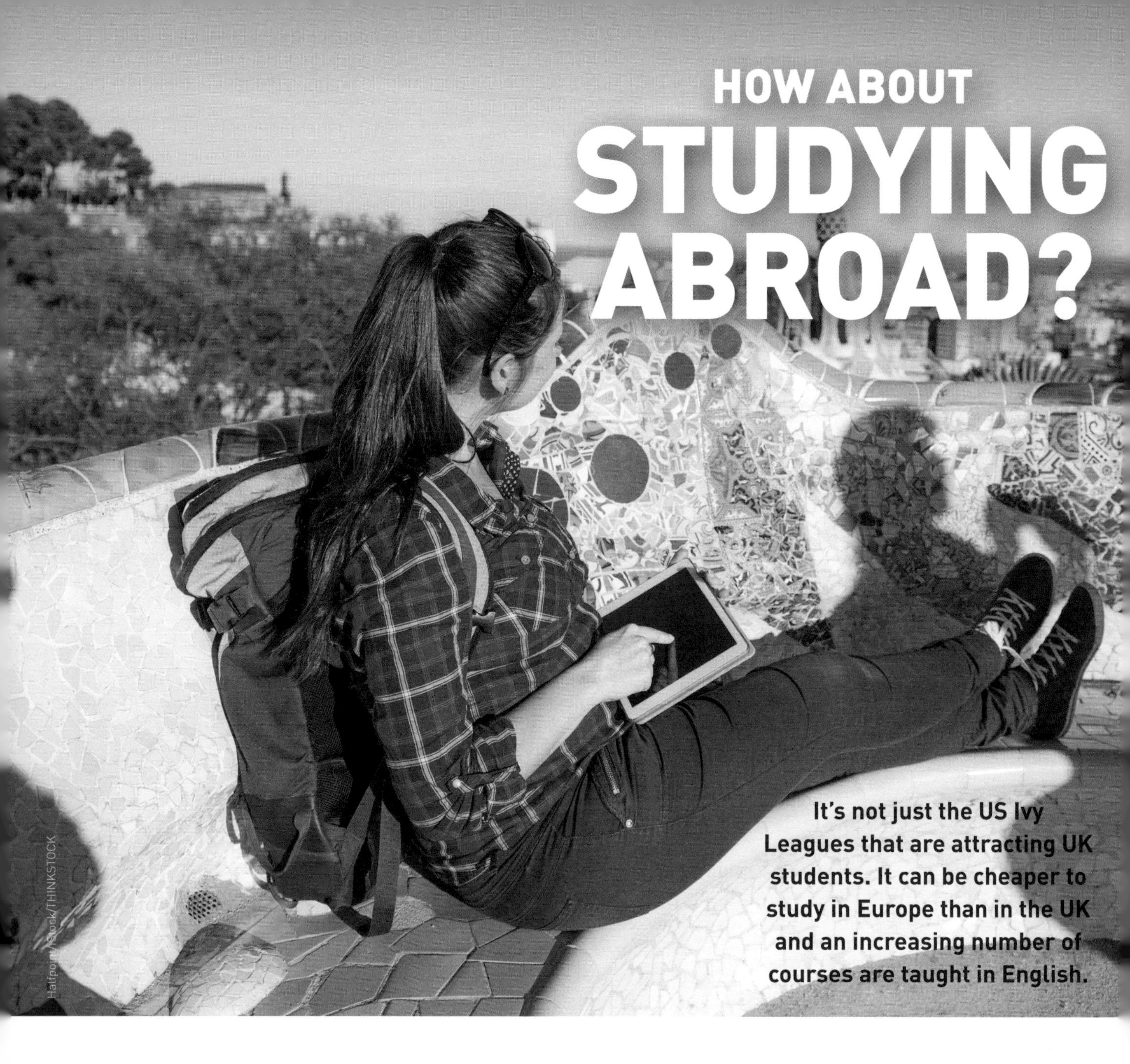

Halfpoint/iStock/THINKSTOCK

HOW ABOUT STUDYING ABROAD?

It's not just the US Ivy Leagues that are attracting UK students. It can be cheaper to study in Europe than in the UK and an increasing number of courses are taught in English.

In recent years the number of UK students applying to universities outside the UK has rapidly increased. A driving factor has been rising tuition fees in the UK which have resulted in students looking elsewhere for less expensive higher education options. The increase in the cost of a UK university education has also reduced the relative cost of higher education in places such as the USA, Canada and Australia, making these attractive alternatives. Some European countries, which traditionally charge considerably less than the UK for undergraduate education, have introduced more courses delivered in English to meet demand. It's not all about finances though: in an increasingly globalised world, students recognise the benefits of living in another country and immersing themselves in a different culture, with the opportunity to learn and develop fluency in another language and gain international work experience.

The top 100 places in the QS World University Rankings 2015/16 are dominated by US and UK institutions but they also feature a number of European institutions, including the University of Heidelberg (66), the University of Copenhagen (69) and Trinity College Dublin (79).

How transferable are the degrees?

Within the European Union, university degrees are recognised by a common system of academic credits called ECTS credits. These are cumulative and transferable, meaning it should be straightforward to move between institutions. It is also a standard system, enabling employers to assess equivalence of qualifications.

> **THIS MAY HELP**
>
> **For more information on US degree courses and the application process, visit the Fulbright Commission website.**

> **THIS MAY HELP**
>
> **The Good Schools Guide publishes 'Uni in the USA and Beyond', a handbook written by students for students full of college profiles and inside information on studying abroad.**

USA

With over 4,500 US colleges offering undergraduate programmes potential students are spoilt for choice—from large campus universities to single sex liberal arts colleges and sprawling city based institutions.

Undergraduate courses in the US are taken over four years and are traditionally flexible, with students studying a wide range of subjects in the first two years prior to selecting a major. Unlike the UK where students apply to read a particular subject at university, students apply to a college in the US and are expected to play an active role in contributing to college life. Therefore, both academic profile and extracurricular activities are important elements of the application.

The cost of an undergraduate course in the US is generally higher than in the UK; fees vary significantly between universities and the cost of living can vary by location. Public universities are generally less expensive than private ones but as they have been established with the intention of educating children from that particular state, the acceptance levels for international students can be low. As a guide, an undergraduate degree at a public university will cost c. £13,000 per annum and at a private university c. £20,000. Many universities provide financial assistance and scholarships are available to international applicants.

> **THE INSIDE TRACK**
>
> "Studying overseas for one or more years of one's degree suggests a get-up-and-go mentality that I like. However, I do have a natural inclination towards degrees issued by a UK university. It's not that I doubt the quality of education overseas; it's merely that I don't know how to compare like for like. I would advise those who wish to study abroad to make sure it's easy for potential employers to understand their degree qualification."
>
> **NICK, DIRECTOR OF A PUBLISHING COMPANY**

Europe

Increasing numbers of UK students are choosing to apply to European universities, attracted by the quality of the education on offer for little or no cost and the opportunity to experience another culture and language. In addition many universities throughout Europe offer a wide range of courses taught in English.

Fee levels across the area differ, state sector institutions in Switzerland and Austria charge below €1,500 per annum, while in the Netherlands fees are at a level of c. €1,900 per annum. There are currently no tuition fees incurred by UK students applying to universities in the four Scandinavian countries.

Although tuition fee loan schemes ▶

OneInchPunch/iStock/THINKSTOCK

A STUDENT SPEAKS

ATTENDING A US UNIVERSITY

"At a US university you will be infinitely challenged and stretched, which is terrifying but also extremely rewarding. Apply to a university that will suit you best in terms of your personality and goals. However, enter university with an open mind. This includes your intended major, and expectations on academic and social life. Don't be afraid to try something new (I took a jazz class which is why I am pursuing a music minor, but also loved my class on German expressionism), and don't be afraid to fail (I interviewed for four clubs and was accepted to only one during my freshmen year, but am now VP of three clubs). It is important to be honest with yourself and pursue things that you truly enjoy. Lastly, you will have so much fun!"

Freshman, Penn University

are available in most EU countries, they are not required to provide financial assistance on the same basis to individuals from other member states unless they have been living in the country for at least five years prior to the start of their studies. In some European countries, however, there is some support available to students: for example, in the Netherlands, student loans will cover the full cost of tuition and non-repayable grants are also available for those in part-time employment. As well as living costs, which can vary significantly depending on location, most universities require students to have medical and liability insurance.

THIS MAY HELP

Further information on opportunities available in Europe is available on the Eunicas website. Eunicas is an independent application support service and does not charge universities for listing their programmes on its website.

Australia and New Zealand

Australia and New Zealand also attract interest from UK students; language and the lifestyle are a great draw. Both countries are home to a number of internationally acclaimed

universities and have education systems established on the UK model. Degree qualifications are recognised everywhere as the direct equivalent of a UK university degree.

Erasmus and other options

If your son or daughter is interested in spending a period of study abroad, one of the most cost-effective ways to achieve this is via an exchange programme. Students must be enrolled on a course at a UK university and apply for an exchange place to undertake part of their studies (usually a year) overseas. One of the best-known exchange schemes is the Erasmus programme, an initiative of the European Union that is run by the British Council in the UK.

Students are not required to pay tuition fees to the university abroad and the fees due to their UK university are currently waived for the period they are overseas, on the condition that the period of study is a full academic year of 24 weeks. Students can still benefit from student loans in the UK and may even be able to obtain grants to help with their costs. In addition, those participating in an Erasmus programme may also receive a grant from the European Commission to cover the additional costs associated with living abroad. ■

THIS MAY HELP

Study Options is the official Application Support Service for students in the UK interested in applying to many Australian and New Zealand universities. They provide free independent advice to students to help them choose the right course at the right university.

Viktor Cap/iStock/THINKSTOCK

ATTENDING AN AUSTRALIAN UNIVERSITY

"Studying in Australia is very similar to studying in the UK, except with better weather in between classes. A lot of the students in Melbourne where I'm studying are international, which means we're all in the same boat. The grading system in Australia is different—but that is really the only significant difference I noticed. (Other than that you don't get palm trees on campus in the UK!) The great thing about studying in Australia is that, although you do feel far away from home, there is no language barrier—which makes it all seem less foreign. The culture here is pretty similar to British culture, which makes it an easy and familiar place to move to."

Annie, Global Media Communication student at University of Melbourne

Parenting

monkeybusinessimages/iStock/THINKSTOCK

As parents we are programmed to see potential problems rather than possibilities; it's easy to forget about or undervalue the optimism of youth. Try and think back to how you felt when you were at a similar stage—what advice did you value? What didn't you want to hear? Ultimately the choice of university must be your child's decision. Even if they go ahead against your best judgement there comes a time when you must step back and accept their choice. Your son or daughter needs to be confident that you are still willing and able to listen or help should anything go wrong.

BE HONEST ABOUT YOUR HOPES

Change can mean new friends, and while you obviously want the best for your child and above all for them to be happy, you may also want them to be successful, have a good job, have financial independence (important given the level of student debt) and achieve status in life.

ASK YOURSELF...

Am I worried about what other people think?

MAKE COMPROMISES

You may have your heart set on your child attending an elite university; they have other intentions. With five choices on the UCAS form there is room for compromise and, indeed, it is worth applying for a lower-ranked university to secure a reasonable place.

ASK YOURSELF...

Am I comparing my child's choice of university to that of friends' children?

RESPECT YOUR CHILD'S KNOWLEDGE

Remember that things are different from when you were at school. The reputations of universities are constantly changing and your child and their school will probably know much more about this than you and friends do, especially the ones who think they are so well informed about everything to do with universities!

ASK YOUR CHILD...

Can you visualise yourself living here?

Teacher and pupil at Felsted School

WHAT DOES MY CHILD NEED TO DO BEFORE APPLYING?

The actual process of applying should not be too daunting for a well-organised student—but don't underestimate the amount of work involved.

Once applicants have chosen the right course and university, the next hurdle is writing a Personal Statement (**see p. 54**). Few of us are adept at selling ourselves and your child will need help and support to do this effectively.

If your child is hoping to go to Oxford or Cambridge, or they are applying for medical and related subjects, there may be specialist tests and interviews. Schools should be taking a lead in providing the extra teaching needed; your job is to maintain a supportive environment in which your child can prepare and reinforce what their school is doing.

Finally you should not forget that in the end, exam results will be the main deciding factor. Important though the intricacies of university application may be, it is A level, Pre-U or IB results which will make all the difference, and the application process should not in any way be a distraction from school work and focus on exam performance.

How the school should help

School students can be reluctant to communicate with you about how their academic work is going, whether good or bad: the shrugged comment of 'OK', 'Fine' or 'Don't worry' hardly provides the basis on which to give informed support. A parents' evening is an opportunity to talk with teachers, tutors or advisors to gain a realistic view of the situation. Alternatively you can make a special appointment with the relevant members of staff. Your child must be involved in the discussion; you definitely don't want to give the impression you are working behind their back and it is important that any mutual concerns are aired and resolved as early as possible. Don't forget that, in some respects, the school will know your child better than you do. ■

PREPARATION AT SCHOOL

"My school guided us every step of the way with the application process—from rigorous checks of our Personal Statements to mock interviews and even general discussion groups for those applying to Oxbridge. I have them to thank for my place at Durham."

Alex, Modern Languages student at Durham

WHAT MAKES AN APPLICANT LOOK GOOD ON PAPER?

Your child may be absolutely charming and fascinating to talk to, but they first need to stand out on paper.

Jetta Productions/DigitalVision/THINKSTOCK

The first impression a university will have of your child will come from a load of paperwork: the Personal Statement (**see p. 54**); the school reference; their CV. Many applicants will never be called to interview; your child may well need to earn their university place by looking impressive on paper.

Extracurricular activities

The UCAS system offers plenty of space for applicants to fill out a CV of work experience and extracurricular activities. Time was when these extracurricular activities could earn them a university place, but things have changed dramatically, and universities are primarily—if not exclusively—concerned with an applicant's academic potential rather than their wider interests. This is particularly true of Oxbridge where tutors don't want their students spending too much time on sport, music, drama or debating.

That said, universities are keen to recruit young people who are interesting and have enthusiasms, particularly if these can be linked to their proposed area of study or provide an enterprising contrast.

They like to see evidence of things such as good time-management, initiative, team-work and leadership

THE INSIDE TRACK

"We don't just want a list of the committees you are on, or the sports or musical instruments you play. We are interested in how your activities have helped you develop skills or qualities that will make you a good student."

WARWICK UNIVERSITY

altrendo images/Stockbyte/THINKSTOCK

THE INSIDE TRACK

"All admissions decisions are based on academic criteria, and excellence in an extracurricular activity will never compensate for lower academic potential."

CAMBRIDGE UNIVERSITY

6 WAYS TO **BOOST YOUR CV**

1 **Read** more widely on aspects of your chosen subject, especially those not in your exam syllabus.

2 Go to **lectures, conferences and taster-days** related to your subject.

3 Undertake relevant **work experience**. This does not have to be glamorous or high-powered: medical schools like applicants who have perhaps worked in a care-home or hospice; applicants for Law might spend some time in a legal advice centre.

4 Make sure you are well informed on **current issues** and aspects of your chosen subject in the news. Universities like students who know about the world they live in.

5 Take part in **school activities** such as sport, music and drama.

6 Take part in **essay competitions** and other competitive academic challenges.

which may not always be evident from an applicant's academic profile. They also appreciate individuals who are community-minded and play a role in the wider world.

While yomping through muddy fields carrying a tent is certainly character building, D of E or similar activities may fail to impress admissions staff. Something that can make a difference is music. Achieving grades seven, eight or above in one or more instruments demonstrates that you are dedicated and well organised enough to do your academic work and hours of music practice.

The school reference

The school reference will be almost entirely about their academic aptitude, with a little on wider interests and contributions to school life. By your child's final year, they will not be able to reinvent themselves (and nor should they wish to) merely to get a better reference from the school—but there is certainly no harm in making an extra effort to prove their capability and dedication. ■

Pupils in the mixed sixth form at Sevenoaks School

THE INSIDE TRACK

"The UCAS Academic Reference plays a very important role in our decision making process. We use it to assess not only the student's current achievements but also their future potential."
MANCHESTER UNIVERSITY

AUTHOR'S TIPS

5 WAYS TO GET A **BETTER** SCHOOL REFERENCE

1 **Work hard**, and respond positively to guidance from teachers.

2 Be aware of the topics in which they need to **focus** their efforts.

3 **Organise** time effectively, especially when it comes to coursework.

4 Participate actively in class **discussion**; universities want open, questioning minds which challenge conventional wisdom.

5 Take up suggestions for **extension work** to follow up interests not covered in the curriculum; universities like those whose interests go beyond the sixth form course and who show intellectual initiative.

WHAT MAKES A GOOD PERSONAL STATEMENT?

The UCAS website tells applicants 'You can write up to 4000 characters of text that shows you'd make a great student'—easier said than done for most sixth-formers.

For many students the Personal Statement can be the most daunting part of the application process and one for which they need greatest support and guidance. The Personal Statement has to demonstrate enthusiasm, ability, knowledge, understanding, commitment, aptitude, a willingness to learn and individuality. All of this has to be supported by evidence and expressed with a subtle balance between confidence and modesty: universities want students who are aware of their strengths but who are equally keen to extend their knowledge and understanding through three or more years of intensive study.

One Personal Statement must serve for all five courses to which students can apply through UCAS. This can produce problems if they are applying for different courses at different universities or for joint courses. As a result, a few universities (for example, Durham and Cambridge) encourage applicants to submit a supplementary Personal Statement which just focuses on the course at that university.

It is hardly surprising that so many students baulk at the task, leave it to the last minute or resort to models from Internet sites—and it is worth mentioning at this stage that UCAS has anti-plagiarism software: the whole application could be invalidated if the Personal Statement is not personal.

THE INSIDE TRACK

"Admissions tutors want to see evidence that applicants have researched the course content and are enthusiastic about studying the course. Your child can demonstrate enthusiasm by including details of what they like about the course, what their key interests within the subject are, and how studying the subject fits in with their long term plans. Where possible, they should be specific—for example, rather than saying they like the course, say specifically what they like about the course."

BATH UNIVERSITY

Most teenagers are not used to selling themselves in this way and often come across as either too self-effacing or assertively arrogant. Things are not helped by the British reluctance to blow one's own trumpet and a distaste for overconfidence; apply to a US College and you can say how brilliant you are in no uncertain terms. UK universities on the other hand prefer calm moderation and a more reserved approach where over-the-top declarations of passion are likely to be treated with suspicion. In fact deleting the phrase 'I am passionate about' entirely from one's Personal Statement is strongly advised.

Jacob Ammentorp Lund/iStock/THINKSTOCK

In the end, an Admissions Tutor simply needs to be convinced by a Personal Statement that this is someone to whom it is worth offering a place, someone who will benefit from what the university has to offer, who will be stimulating to teach and who will make the fullest contribution to university life. A tall order—yes, but with a little help, your child will be able to present themselves effectively.

Catch their attention

In their first trawl, most universities will not spend more than ten minutes on each UCAS form. To stand out, a Personal Statement must be original and well written. It should convince anyone of the applicant's genuine interest in a subject and show evidence of academic reading (name books) and thinking beyond the syllabus. General skills (research, writing etc), work experience and hobbies should be included if they are demonstrably relevant to the course.

The opening is by far the most difficult part to write: it should be arresting and original but ▶

Impressive openings for Personal Statements

History

Only three of my great-great-great grandparents' thirteen children survived to adulthood. It was certainly not uncommon for this to be the case for a working class family in the nineteenth century due to the living conditions and environment in a 'stuff warehouse' in Bradford. Researching my family this summer, which took me from the online censuses to the parish microfiche in Yorkshire, I discovered how directly they had been affected: this new found relationship to what had before been abstract fact encapsulated what history is ultimately about for me: the study of human beings and how they think, feel and behave. This interest in humanity and its past is why I want to study History at university.

Law

At the Old Bailey this summer I saw a London bus driver acquitted of killing a man. The driver did not break the speed limit nor was he driving recklessly. Yes he could have braked, but he made the decision that the pedestrian posed no threat. Should he be punished for this? The prosecution based its argument on the principle that breaking the law should not go unchallenged; had the main point about braking been successfully argued, the driver could have been charged with manslaughter. What interests me most about the law is that legal questions do not always have clearly defined answers.

Seniors at Felsted learn about printing

Digital Vision/Photodisc/THINKSTOCK

suitably scholarly and relevant to the skills and knowledge needed for the course in question. A short, concise concluding summary or statement will round things off well; two or three lines is quite enough. There is simply not the space for a rambling, involved conclusion.

When to begin

It's a good idea if your child can at least start thinking about the Personal Statement or, even better, produce an initial draft, before the summer holidays. This means they will have the chance to discuss the content more fully and there will be time to address any weaknesses in the application, for example the need for wider reading. Many schools set their own deadlines for completing the Personal Statement to allow for checking and if necessary, redrafting.

Starting a draft

A good way for your child to start is by writing down all the reasons why they want to go to university and what they like about their chosen subject. Some young people find mind maps or spider diagrams useful, some prefer bullet point lists and others prefer to go 'freestyle'. A list of relevant reading, activities and experiences could be added along with a note of what they have learned from each one. Next, this information can be arranged into an overall structure, indicating the purpose of each paragraph and the evidence which might be included in each one. ■

THE INSIDE TRACK

"Personal Statements are often used as a basis for discussion at interview. In a Personal Statement we are looking for applicants to:

- explain their reasons for wanting to study the subject
- demonstrate their enthusiasm for and commitment to their chosen course
- express any particular interests within the field
- outline how they have pursued their interest in the subject in their own time."

CAMBRIDGE UNIVERSITY

10 DOs AND DON'Ts FOR A **GREAT PERSONAL STATEMENT**

DO...

1 Have a logical **structure**: if it helps, plan the text as though it is an essay with the title 'Why should we give you a place to study this subject at our university?'

2 Illustrate motivation, commitment, knowledge, aptitude, analytical skills and **enthusiasm** with precise examples.

3 Provide **evidence** to prove a point.

4 **Be honest;** an applicant should say what they think, not what they think the university wants to hear. Nevertheless, be aware of what the university is looking for and focus comments accordingly.

5 Everything should be **relevant** to the course that is being applied for—even extracurricular interests. If it's a joint course, divide the text into sections for each subject and perhaps discuss the links.

6 Include details which make the applicant **distinctive, interesting and different** from others.

7 When referring to reading, work experience and other activities, applicants should **reflect** on what they learnt and how it increased their understanding of a topic.

8 Use **clear, unpretentious language** without too many adjectives and adverbs or overly complex syntax.

9 Think of a punchy and original **opening and conclusion**; the start and the end of a piece of writing is what people remember most.

10 A Personal Statement is just that: **personal**. It must be the applicant's own work and reflect their true thoughts and opinions.

Jetta Productions/Photodisc/THINKSTOCK

DON'T...

1 Write too little about **academic interests**: at least 75% should be directly about the subject you want to study. Confine hobbies, work experience etc to near the end.

2 Use too many **over-the-top, gushing words** (eg fascinated, relish, enthralled, passionate).

3 Make assertions which are not backed up with **evidence**, particularly if they are about how good the candidate is.

4 **Refer to specific universities**, either directly or by implication.

5 **Plagiarise.** Copying someone else's Personal Statement or downloading one from a website is a cardinal sin. UCAS has sophisticated software to check for this.

6 Use **clichés** or try to be funny. Clichés are a waste of words and jokes are likely to irritate.

7 Make **spelling and grammatical errors**—though there can be problems with foreign languages because of the limitations of the UCAS online system which does not do accents.

8 Use a **convoluted style**, such as lots of subordinate clauses, or beginning paragraphs with participles ('Having been'; 'Attending lectures').

9 Start or end with a pretentious or **over-used** quotation.

10 Start every sentence **with the word 'I'.**

anyaberkut/iStock/THINKSTOCK

Ondine32/iStock/THINKSTOCK

IN THE KNOW

"These are the ten most overused Personal Statement openings. Don't use them!

I am currently studying a BTEC National Diploma in ... (used 464 times)

From a young age I have always been interested in ... (309 times)

From an early age I have always been interested in ... (292 times)

Nursing is a very challenging and demanding career ... (275 times)

For as long as I can remember I have been fascinated with ... (196 times)

"Fashion is not something that exists in dresses only" ... (189 times)

Nursing is a profession I have always looked upon with ... (178 times)

For as long as I can remember I have been interested in ... (166 times)

I am an International Academy student and have been studying since ... (141 times)

Academically, I have always been a very determined and ... (138 times)"

FIGURES FROM UCAS

Great endings for Personal Statements

Business Studies
I am optimistic that this course will prepare me for a wide range of careers and studying the principles and practices of business management at university will be a fantastic platform to provide the life skills to, one day, contribute to a company of any size.

Engineering
I believe I am ideally suited to Engineering: I love to design and build, and have thoroughly enjoyed my exposure to the subject so far. I am looking forward to an inspiring and challenging course at university where I can be stretched to my full potential.

Parenting

Cathy Yeulet/iStock/THINKSTOCK

Normally laid-back teenagers who nonchalantly seem to take everything in their stride can become fraught at the prospect of starting their university application—and stress levels will only be compounded by over-anxious parents. It is essential to tread cautiously, be constantly supportive and ensure that your input is presented positively and as suggestions: you do not necessarily know best and, even if you do, your child may not think so. If your child refuses all offers of help, withdrawal is the best policy—but be alert for any subsequent requests for help, however oblique.

STEP BACK

Resist the urge to take over and ghost write your child's application. Universities can usually detect the hand of over-involved parents, and are more likely to favour straight talking which is obviously the work of the applicant—even if it seems a little unsophisticated.

HAND OVER TO THE SCHOOL

Teachers are in a better position to provide direct criticism which will not be emotionally charged! If there is conflicting advice and opinion, try to reconcile the differences without undermining the school.

ASK YOURSELF...

Am I confident that my child will take advice from the school, if not from me?

WHAT YOUR CHILD MAY BE WORRYING ABOUT

- How do I write positively about myself?
- I have so much I want to say. How do I get it down to 4,000 characters?
- Have I got enough to say about myself to fill up the 4,000 characters?
- How do I write about a subject I've never studied?
- I am not brilliant at writing. Will that do me down?

ASK YOURSELF...

What skills do I have which might be of use to my child in writing a Personal Statement?

TALK IT THROUGH

It's a good idea for you and your child to discuss their achievements together, both academic and broader. This will help them feel confident starting the Personal Statement, and will also ensure all relevant information is included. It is advisable to communicate these achievements to the referee at school as well, though you cannot control what is included in the reference.

DON'T PUSH IT

Even if you're sure you have good advice to pass on, present it only as a suggestion, and do not push it. Adolescent pride being what it is, having ostensibly rejected your suggestions, your child may quietly adopt them.

HOW DOES THE APPLICATION PROCESS WORK?

The UCAS online application is accessed through UCAS Apply. Most teenagers will have no problem using this website.

Completing the application itself is usually very simple. Applications are made through UCAS Apply, which is available on the UCAS website, and which most students should find intuitive and easy to use. Working their way carefully through each section of the application using the guidance notes and videos provided by UCAS will help your child navigate the process with ease.

The majority of applicants will need only to submit the one application to UCAS Apply. However there are a few exceptions: if your child is applying to a foundation course at an art college, they will probably need to apply to each college directly. Applications for specialist performing arts colleges, such as RADA, may also need to be directed to individual institutions. Eight colleges (including the leading music colleges) now have a common application system: UCAS Conservatoires (formerly CUKAS).

Your child can usually apply to independent colleges (eg New College of the Humanities; University of Buckingham; Regent's University) through UCAS, but there may also be an direct application system. If your child uses the direct option, they can apply to such institutions in addition to their five UCAS choices and applications often remain open well after the UCAS 15th January deadline. This is a good option if your child is not getting the offers they want without having to go through UCAS Extra.

Registration

Your son or daughter will first have to register with UCAS Apply in order to start completing their application. Most sections are very straightforward to complete, particularly for resident students who are at school in the UK. For international students, the process can be more complicated.

For example, some applicants are confused by the request for their postal address and home address: these are likely to be identical for UK pupils living at home, so it is only necessary to complete the postal address section. Overseas students at boarding school may wish to have any UCAS or university correspondence sent to their school and, in this case, should add the school address as their postal address. It is important to remember to change these details when they leave school to ensure correspondence is received punctually.

Peter M Fisher/Fuse/THINKSTOCK

Logging in

When your son or daughter logs in to Apply the first time, they will be asked a number of questions, as well as asked for a buzzword which has been provided by the school, which will enable them to link their application to their school. This will enable the school to add the UCAS reference and predicted grades and also to review their application before it is submitted—by the school—to UCAS.

A 10 digit UCAS Personal ID will then be issued. This is a very important reference as it will need to be quoted in all correspondence with UCAS and the universities included in the application.

Filling out the application

Students can fill out the application in any order; it is not necessary to complete a section fully before moving on to the next. However, before leaving a section, it is important to save the information to ensure it is not lost. When a section has been completed in full, the 'section completed' button needs to be checked before clicking 'save' to ensure the menu registers the section is complete. There is also a 'cancel' option to start the section again.

Your child can nominate a parent, guardian or advisor to contact UCAS regarding their application on their behalf. This can be very helpful if, for example, they are planning to be away on a gap year when they apply or when results are released.

International students

International students will be presented with a number of additional questions. They will be asked for a reference number, which can be left blank if irrelevant to them, or used to include the relevant reference of their English language qualification, such as an IELTS or TOEFL reference (taken from the bottom of their certificate). If they need a visa to study in the UK, they will need to fill out their passport details.

Disabled/special needs students

Students who have a disability or special need (such as dyslexia or dyspraxia) have the opportunity to declare this. Although there is often a reluctance to provide this information, it is best to do so, as it will enable their chosen universities to ensure any additional support they may require is available to them, e.g. use of a laptop. This information has no influence on the assessment of their application. Students who have no disability should select 'no disability' from the drop-down box as it cannot be left blank.

None of the universities will know to which other universities your child has applied until they have replied to their offers—and so universities will therefore not be influenced by your child's other choices when they are assessing their application. There is no ranking implied in the way your child lists their choices.

Student finance

Students are asked to indicate if they intend to apply for student finance or if they will be privately financing their degree. UCAS doesn't arrange the finance but your child can give ▶

THE INSIDE TRACK

"Common errors include making mistakes on the point of entry, for example not putting the correct starting year. Students don't always include qualifications which they are currently undertaking or qualifications which they are retaking. A complete application form impresses, as well as students expressing passion in their application."

MIDDLESEX UNIVERSITY

Jetta Productions/Photodisc/THINKSTOCK

permission for them to share their information with the Student Loans Company if they plan to apply for student finance, which can help to speed up this process. Your child's application will not be affected by the way they answer this question and they can change their mind about applying for finance at a later date. There is an opportunity to sign up for email notifications regarding student finance arrangements.

Qualifications

Applicants should set out all their school qualifications to date; if they choose, they can even enter individual module results, but it is advisable to be consistent about this. If they have not yet received their AS level certificates, but have strong results, they should enter these as 'pending'. Some universities may ask for details of these scores anyway if they are not included in the form. Details of all final exams to be taken (A level, IB etc) should also be entered as 'pending'.

If your son or daughter did not take GCSEs, the equivalent level qualifications can be found using the extensive list provided. When entering results, the actual grade or mark awarded should be included; your child should not try to convert the qualification into a GCSE grade equivalent.

Submitting the application

Once all sections are complete, it will be possible for your son or daughter to submit their application. This is done using the Pay/Send option. If they are applying through their school or college, it does not go to UCAS when they submit their application in this way. It goes directly to their school or college to add their reference and predicted grades if they have yet to take their final school exams. Only the school or college can send the application. If they are applying as an independent applicant, the UCAS application will go directly to UCAS. ■

7 THINGS TO REMEMBER

1 **For most subjects students can apply for five university courses.**

2 If your child is applying for Medicine, Dentistry, or Veterinary Science/Medicine, they can select up to **four** courses in these subjects but may add a fifth choice in another subject.

3 They may only apply to **Oxford or Cambridge** in the same year.

4 **The London University colleges count as separate choices. Other universities with a collegiate system (eg Durham, York, Kent) have a centralised admission system and an application counts as one UCAS choice.**

5 While almost all universities work through UCAS, some institutions allow direct applications in addition to your child's five UCAS choices (eg University of Buckingham; New College of the Humanities).

6 **Courses for the same subject at different universities may have different course codes, so you need to check these carefully.**

7 For extracurricular qualifications, it is necessary to include only the most recent of each, e.g. if Grade 8 piano has been achieved, it is not necessary to include details of Grades 1–7.

WHAT IS THE APPLICATION PROCESS FOR OXBRIDGE?

Applicants to Oxford or Cambridge will have more to do than most of their peers.

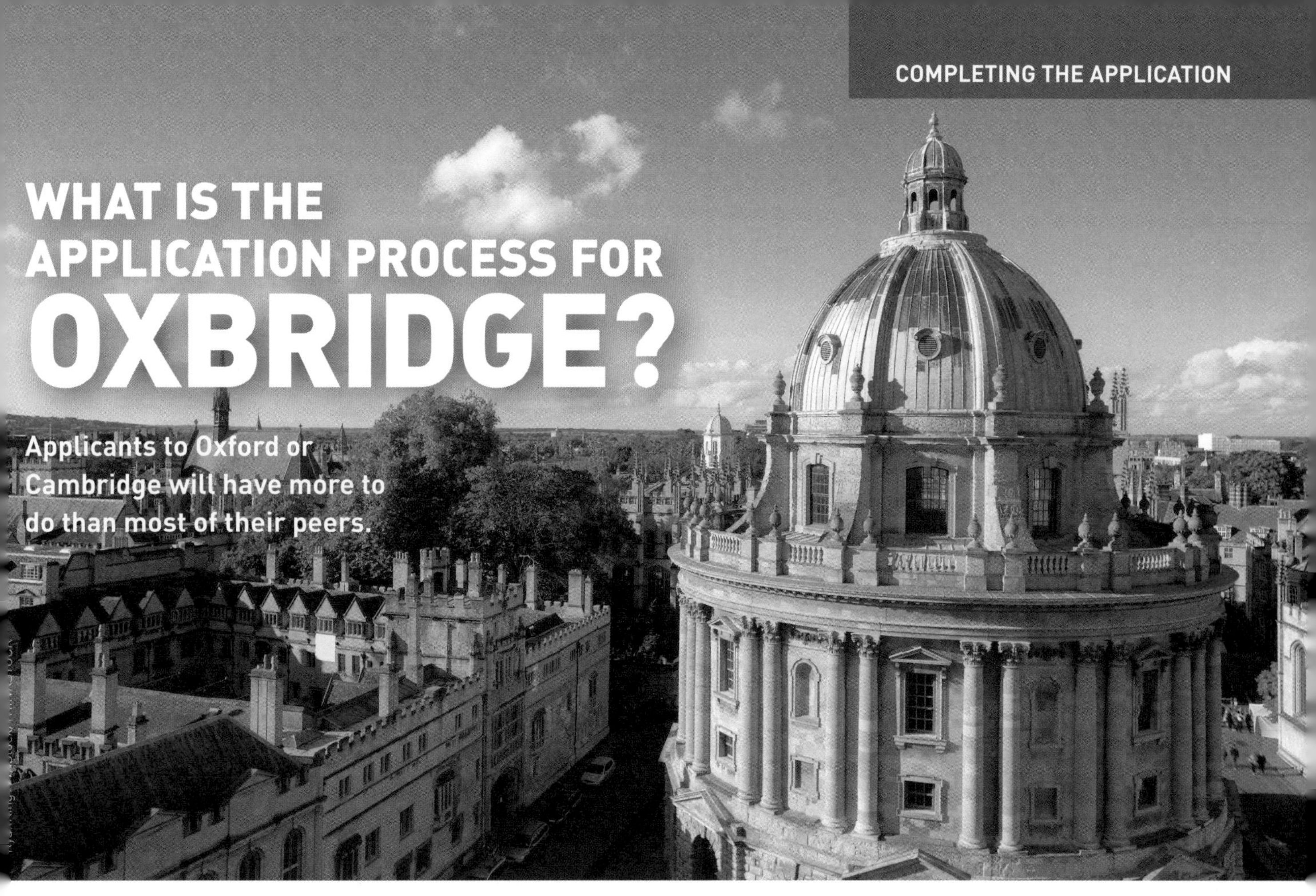

If your child is applying for Oxford or Cambridge, the application process can appear daunting. If your child's school lacks expertise in the field of Oxbridge applications you may have to do more yourself than for other aspects of the UCAS application process. However, with a good support system in place and a willingness to work hard, your child should find the process manageable—and if they are as passionate about their subject as Oxbridge requires, they should enjoy it!

Your child can either specify a college or opt for an open application. Around 20% of applicants opt for this route: it makes no difference to their chance of getting a place and, once allocated, they will be treated like applicants who chose the college. If your child is going for an open application, then they must be certain that they will be happy with being a member of any college.

Subject tests (Oxford)

Oxford requires most applicants to sit a specialist paper. Your child must register to sit these Oxford exams—they will not be automatically entered simply by applying for the appropriate course—but their school may well do this for them. The registration deadline is 15th October, and the tests take place at an exam centre—normally your child's school—in the first week of November.

Aptitude tests, as the name implies, are intended to assess skills and potential; they do not presuppose a body of knowledge and are not a test of facts. They are designed so that candidates from different backgrounds and countries can be assessed fairly.

Applicants may have to take either a specific subject test, or the Oxford Thinking Skills Assessment; applicants for joint courses may need to take tests in both subjects.

Subject tests (Cambridge)

Cambridge is far less consistent in its test requirement. Different colleges have different policies even for the same subject, which is something to take into account when choosing a college.

Many applicants will have to take pre-interview assessment tests, which ▶

THE INSIDE TRACK

"We assess everyone individually, looking for different things in different people. Consequently, there's no magic formula that will guarantee you a place. However, all Admissions Tutors are looking for students with the most academic ability and potential, who are best suited to the course they applied for, and who will benefit from what we have to offer."

CAMBRIDGE UNIVERSITY

Harrenden Biran/Hemera/THINKSTOCK

AUTHOR'S TIPS

6 THINGS TO REMEMBER

1 **Your child can only apply to Oxford or Cambridge and can only apply for one course.**

2 Application is **via UCAS** (see p. 60) and the Oxbridge course counts as one of your child's five choices.

3 **The deadline for submission of a full UCAS application to Oxford or Cambridge is 6.00pm UK time on 15th October.**

4 Those applying to Cambridge must also complete the online **Supplementary Application Questionnaire** (SAQ) which will be sent to them once their application has been received.

5 The deadline for organ and choral **award applications** is earlier, usually in September. Each university has its own system of auditions across colleges.

6 **Your child will be told about the outcome early in January.**

will be held at the applicant's school or an authorised centre. Other subjects will require assessments in Cambridge at the time of interview. Given this diversity of practice, it is crucial to look in detail at the subject-specific section of the website of the college to which your child is applying or has been allocated.

Submission of work

If your child is applying to study one of the humanities or social sciences at either university, they will almost certainly be asked to submit an essay of their choice in the relevant discipline. If they are applying for a subject not being studied at school, then the college will give advice on suitable work to send in. At Oxford there is consistency in these requirements across each subject; at Cambridge each college has its own policy for each subject and the demands vary greatly. The college website gives full information, and the deadline for sending off work is usually the middle of November.

While this work should be an example of normal term-time assignments, and should be directly relevant to the course your child is following, they should do everything they can to ensure that it shows off their ability to the full. The essay has to be marked by a teacher who needs to certify the circumstances under which it was produced and the amount of help given. Your child should also remember that discussion of the submitted work may form part of their interview.

Interviews

Your child's application will be assessed initially on the basis of the school reference, the Personal Statement, their academic profile, the results of specialist tests and the quality of submitted work. If these are up to standard, then your child will be offered an interview in the first two weeks of December. Cambridge interviews most credible applicants, but Oxford has recently reduced the number of applicants interviewed. Interviews are generally based in the first-choice college (or the allocated college for those submitting an open application), but some subjects interview on a faculty basis. At both universities there is a real effort to achieve consistency of assessment in the same subject between colleges. Very occasionally, borderline applicants will be called back for further interviews, but this is uncommon. ■

AUTHOR'S TIPS

IS IT **TOO MUCH** PRESSURE?

Applying to Oxbridge is certainly a lot of work. Interviewers will expect applicants to have immersed themselves in reading and study beyond the A level/IB syllabus, which can be time-consuming.

The school should help with preparation for any specialist tests—and many schools even have interview training programmes. If the school is reluctant to help—and the pressure on teachers' time may prevent personal attention to a single Oxbridge applicant—then it might be good to consult an expert. There are plenty of companies offering training and guidance for a fee, but make sure that they are reputable and know what they are doing.

Overall, an application to Oxbridge is sure to add an element of pressure to your child's final year—but there are plenty of support systems available to ensure this pressure never gets too much.

HERE TO HELP

"The offer of a place will be conditional on high performance in a number of subjects: your child must not focus on their Oxbridge application to the exclusion of other subjects—particularly as a place cannot be guaranteed even for the most able."

CAREERS ADVISOR, BENENDEN SCHOOL

WHAT IS THE PROCESS FOR APPLYING FOR MEDICINE?

Applicants to medical school face a particularly demanding application process.

The UK's 33 medical schools are overwhelmed with applications and only about one in ten of them will be successful. Medicine is also the only subject which has a government-imposed quota limiting the number of international students (at present around 7% of places).

> Only about one in ten medical applicants are successful

If your child is hoping to study medicine it is important to discuss their motives and to make sure they know what is involved: a long and demanding course which attracts highly competitive applicants. It is equally crucial that you talk with them and their school about whether they are going to achieve the necessary grades for entry (at least three As at A level is typical). Medicine is the subject which, perhaps more than any other, becomes the object of tunnel-vision ambition on the part of school students, often encouraged by parental aspirations. Realistic appraisal at an early stage can prevent disappointment becoming too wounding and leaves time to explore equally worthwhile and rewarding alternatives—which might still lead to a career in medicine.

The best applicants are those who combine a real enthusiasm for the science involved in medicine with strength of character and the potential to work in a caring profession. Vague desires to do good and benefit society

Many medical schools recruit graduates in related disciplines, so a failure to get accepted for a first degree in medicine does not necessarily mean the end of your child's ambitions to be a doctor.

have to be supported by the stark reality of academic excellence and the ability to cope with the huge amounts of work involved. Anecdotally, medicine is probably the most highly pressurised of all university subjects and your child has to be able to cope both academically and personally. Most medical schools have very clear non-academic requirements as well; these will be detailed in each university's Admissions Policy Statement, which makes essential reading.

AUTHOR'S TIPS

4 THINGS TO REMEMBER

1 Your child can only apply for four courses in Medicine, Dentistry and Veterinary Medicine/Science. Most applicants use their fifth choice for a related subject (eg Biochemistry; Biological Science; Animal Science).

2 Completed applications have to be submitted to UCAS by **15th October.**

3 The majority of medical schools (26 out of 33) require applicants to take the **UK Clinical Aptitude Test** (UKCAT); a few require the **Biomedical Admissions Test** (BMAT).

4 Only a small portion of applicants will be shortlisted, but almost all of the shortlisted candidates should expect to be called for an **interview** **(see p. 75)** or multiple mini interviews.

UKCAT and BMAT tests

Registration for either the UKCAT or BMAT tests involves payment of a fee. Remember that if your child is applying to a university which requires BMAT, the chances are that they will still need to take the UKCAT for their other choices.

The UKCAT is a computer-based test delivered by Pearson Vue at their high street centres. Your child will get their test result on leaving the test centre. As this will be before the 15 October UCAS deadline, it could influence their application. Each university provides information as to how they use the UKCAT score; it varies considerably between universities. Some universities have a threshold score either for the whole test or for different parts of it. If your child has not performed well then it is worth contacting universities directly to see if there is any point in continuing with an application. Universities to which your child has applied will be informed directly of the results. UKCAT is an aptitude test and so requires no extra teaching or preparation, but it is essential that your child has plenty of opportunity to practise past papers. There are training courses which—at a price—can provide excellent guidance; some schools buy in professional trainers for their candidates.

A few medical schools require applicants to take the Biomedical Admissions Test (BMAT)—at present, Cambridge, Oxford, Imperial, UCL, Leeds, Lancaster and Brighton & Sussex. Candidates sit the test, which consists of a skills assessment, writing task and scientific knowledge section, in November at a test centre (usually their school) and results are released online at the end of the month. As the test takes ▶

STRAIGHT FROM THE HORSE'S MOUTH

"We are looking for examples of core qualities a good doctor might have: communication skills; evidence of concern for the welfare of others; demonstration of being trustworthy and honest. Doctors' lives are busy and challenging, and time management is very important."
ABERDEEN UNIVERSITY

Design Pics/THINKSTOCK

Purestock/THINKSTOCK

AUTHOR'S TIPS

IS IT **TOO MUCH** PRESSURE?

If your child is a credible applicant for medical school then the marginal amount of extra work involved is something they should take in their stride and relish. The extra work basically involves preparation for tests and interviews—mainly in the form of practice, as UKCAT requires no extra subject knowledge, and for interviews it is important that applicants are not over-prepared. BMAT preparation will require a bit more learning, but your child's school should provide the academic support they need.

place after the application deadline, the result will be used by universities as part of an overall assessment. BMAT is more knowledge-based than UKCAT and the website has details of what candidates should know, something to which schools should actively respond. Again, there are commercially-run courses available.

Work experience

Work experience is essential for anyone applying to study medicine. While time spent with doctors and surgeons in a hospital can be inspirational and provide real insights, work experience does not have to be high profile. Indeed, medical schools rather like applicants to be aware of the less glamorous side of medicine, for example, through working in a care home, caring for people who are disabled, or volunteering in a health advice centre. What is most important is not the actual work undertaken but what the applicant has learned from it. Almost all voluntary work can contribute to the strength of an application, whether or not the work is specifically medical in tone.

The Personal Statement will be important and should indicate how your child has built a foundation of skill and knowledge to study medicine, with reference to specific areas of medical interest, personal initiatives and work experience. ■

IN THE KNOW

"The test does not contain any curriculum or science content. It focuses on exploring the cognitive powers of candidates and other attributes considered to be valuable for healthcare professionals."
UKCAT

KatarzynaBialasiewicz/iStock/THINKSTOCK

WHAT IS THE APPLICATION PROCESS FOR UNIVERSITIES ABROAD?

Depending on where your child wishes to apply, they may face a number of extra steps.

The application process for overseas universities differs vastly depending on the institution and its location. Some accept applications through a centralised online system (similar to UCAS), whilst others require applications to be submitted directly to the university or college. It is essential that your child checks the application requirements and deadlines on the individual university websites. In comparison to UCAS, the application process to US universities and colleges is considerably more comprehensive and more time-consuming. However, arguably a greater degree of time is spent on assessing each application, so the additional effort required can be very worthwhile.

USA

The application process to universities in the USA differs significantly from the UK. Over 450 US institutions use the Common Application, which allows applicants to submit information and essays to multiple universities. However, approximately one third of universities ask for additional information and/or essays. The application is detailed and the information and essays form a crucial element of the assessment process. Considerable care and attention needs to be taken as applications need to be tailored towards each individual institution.

Unlike UCAS, there is no limit on the number of applications that may be submitted; however, as each application involves individualised information in some form it is generally recommended to complete between six and eight applications. Letters of recommendation from your child's school also form an important element of the application so they should speak to staff about preparing and submitting these.

In addition, many universities and certainly the principal institutions (Yale, Harvard, Princeton etc) also require applicants to complete admissions tests (SAT or ACT). These aptitude tests are designed essentially for US high school students so it is essential for UK students to practise. The tests can be taken multiple times and some universities will accept the best scores in each section from a

Schools can help students decide whether studying abroad is for them. Pic: St Martha's School

range of tests (referred to as super-scoring). However, it is recommended that applicants do not take the test too many times. The suggested timing to take the test for the first time is the autumn term of the Lower Sixth. Although universities do not have specific minimum score requirements, competition for places (especially international places at the top schools) is intense and successful applicants usually have SAT scores in the high 700s in each section.

> **THIS MAY HELP**
>
> **The Good Schools Guide publishes 'Uni in the USA'. It's full of useful information and student reviews of many of the most popular US colleges and universities. The book is written in conjunction with the US-UK Fulbright Commission, the UK's official source of information on US higher education. (See p. 43 for details.)**

US universities and colleges take a holistic approach in assessing applications—as such, it is not just academic credentials and potential that matter but extracurricular interests and activities are also vitally important. Your child should be able to demonstrate initiative and leadership in their wider interests and to illustrate how they will benefit the community they wish to join. Undergraduate courses in the USA are considerably more flexible than most UK degrees and in the first two years your child will study a variety of subjects before selecting a 'major' field in which to specialise. As such, it will be helpful for your child to demonstrate in their application a desire to broaden their intellectual horizons and an open-minded approach to new disciplines.

There are two application routes: regular decision, when applications are due in late December of the year before entry; and early action/decision (available for some universities), when applications are due in mid-November in the year before entry. Care should be taken over the terms of the application process; early decision applications are binding so you and your child will be contractually committed to accept this place should it be offered by the university.

Europe

Entry requirements are generally lower than those set by UK universities, a reflection of the supply of places and student demand, rather than quality. Application deadlines vary between universities so it is important to check individual websites. Similarly, the application process needs to be confirmed as some universities operate a centralised online system whilst others accept only direct applications. Eunicas (European Universities Central Application Support Service) enables UK and Irish students to apply for up to eight degree courses, taught through English, in a number of universities across Europe. The Eunicas website

Halfpoint/iStock/THINKSTOCK

also includes advice and guidance on key areas, including choosing a course, the application process and visa arrangements.

Unlike the USA, applicants to European universities are unlikely to have to complete additional admissions tests, unless applying for courses such as medicine, dentistry and veterinary medicine/science, which might require an aptitude test similar to the UKCAT or BMAT. Applicants for practical or performance related courses may have to submit a portfolio of work or attend an audition, although this will vary by institution.

THIS MAY HELP

Study Options will support students through the application process, from making an application to accepting an offer of a place, and assist with practicalities including student accommodation and student visas.

Australia and New Zealand

Applications are made directly to universities and there is no maximum number of applications. Moving away to study in Australia and New Zealand can be challenging and will require a level of independence and initiative. In addition, Australian and New Zealand degrees are assessed continually from the first year of study and these academic results count towards the final degree. This differs from the system in most UK universities where results in the second and third years of a three-year degree are used to determine the final degree classification. However, away from academic study, there is the opportunity to enjoy the outdoor lifestyles typical of these countries.

Study Options is the official application support service for students in the UK wishing to apply for university courses in Australia and New Zealand and processes applications to institutions within this region. Although applications can also be made directly, Study Options will review these prior to submission and highlight any areas that require amendment or additional attention, which can ultimately save time. ■

"The first thing to say about studying abroad is that the student really must want to. Our son had been very keen and had undertaken his own research; once we decided this was the route that should be encouraged, we went to the Fulbright Exhibition in Kensington where US universities pitch themselves for future students. Once our son had picked his top three, we went to visit the campuses—which was quite expensive, but we made it our summer holiday. The trip really helped us decide on the perfect place for our son to study."

SALLY AND JOHN, WHOSE SON IS STUDYING GLOBAL POLITICS AND BUSINESS AT ARIZONA STATE UNIVERSITY

Parenting

Jonathan Ross/Hemera/THINKSTOCK

Once the choices of course and university have been made and the Personal Statement written, the actual application process is relatively undemanding and consequently unstressful—largely the technical work of feeding the information on to the UCAS form. If your child is dragging their feet over their UCAS application, see if you can find out why without seeming to nag. It could just be the usual teenage brinksmanship but perhaps the process of focusing on higher education and careers has given them pause for thought.

JUST BE THERE

Reluctance to complete the application form may be symptomatic of deeper concerns or serious doubts as to whether this is the right thing for them: this could be a signal for deeper discussion of whether applying to university is what they want to do at this stage or of specific concerns.

WHAT YOUR CHILD MAY BE WORRYING ABOUT

- I am committing myself to three years studying a particular subject at university which may well determine the rest of my life. Have I got it right?
- I am finding this really difficult—but I am not going to ask for help because I'm meant to be a grown-up now and don't want them thinking they know best.

LIFT YOUR CHILD'S CONFIDENCE

At such a stressful time in their lives, it wouldn't be totally unusual for your child to doubt their own intentions half way through the process. Find an opportunity to ask your child if they still feel committed to their original plan—or if they need you to help them change course. If your child isn't bringing this up themselves, do take note that reluctance to complete the application may be symptomatic of deeper concerns or doubts.

DON'T NAG

Talk through a timetable with your child and agree together on reasonable deadlines. This way, they can't feel that you're imposing your own schedule on them. Remember: some people actually find it easier leaving things to the last minute. On the other hand, for some children a brusque "Let's just sit down together and get it done" is exactly what's needed.

ASK YOURSELF...

Is there a point where my concerns are such that I need to get in touch with school?

ASK YOURSELF...

Knowing what my child is like, what are the tactics best designed to avoid confrontation and the appearance of nagging?

WHAT RESPONSES MIGHT UNIVERSITIES GIVE?

The responses can be a little more complicated than a simple acceptance or rejection.

When a university makes a decision about your child's university application, UCAS will email them to advise that there has been a change in the status of their application. At this stage, they don't know what the change is so this can be a rather tense few minutes whilst they log in to UCAS Track using their Personal ID and password. Your son or daughter will receive one of the following messages: conditional offer; unconditional offer; interview; unsuccessful; withdrawn.

Conditional offer

This means they have been offered a place at the university for the course detailed, subject to certain conditions (grades/UCAS points and maybe additional terms, for example certain grades required in particular subjects).

Universities may offer a place on a course other than the one for which your child has applied. Therefore it is essential that these details, together with the offer letter that will also be available in UCAS Track, are carefully reviewed and all conditions noted/met. Some conditions will have deadlines attached, which must also be met, otherwise the offer can be withdrawn.

Unconditional offers

This means they have been offered a confirmed place at the university on the course indicated and there are no further conditions to be met. However, there may be a requirement to submit certain information so it is essential that the detail of the offer is reviewed with care.

Unconditional offers are usually ▶

made if your son or daughter has already completed their final secondary school examinations, e.g. A levels, IB etc. In some cases, students who have still to complete these exams will be offered an unconditional place if they accept the offer as their first or Firm choice. If they choose to accept another offer as their first or Firm choice, the offer will be conditional on certain grades or other terms. Again, it is very important to review the details carefully.

Interviews

If the university wishes to invite your son or daughter for interview prior to making a decision, they may communicate this via UCAS Track and the information will appear on their account. Alternatively, your child may be invited for an audition or to submit work, such as a portfolio or an essay. Usually the university will email details of the interview/audition/work arrangements and these should be carefully read, and dates and timings recorded where appropriate.

Your child will be required to reply to this invitation otherwise the offer of an interview could be revoked and their application will not progress further. If the date proposed does not suit, there is the facility to amend this to an alternative, but it would be best to contact the university to explain their (very good) reason and to ask if this is acceptable. Needless to say, an invitation to an Oxbridge interview should not be amended!

Unsuccessful

This means they have not been offered a place at the university. Some brief feedback comments may be included but this is not usually detailed. If your son or daughter would like additional feedback, they should contact the university to ask if this might be possible.

pixelheadphoto/iStock/THINKSTOCK

Withdrawn

A university can change your son or daughter's status to withdrawn if they have not replied to emails/letters, invitations to interview/audition or submission of work, or failed to attend an interview/audition or submit requested work.

If your son or daughter has not yet received a decision from a university and they are no longer interested in a place on the course, they can withdraw themselves from the course, either by contacting the university or by withdrawing in UCAS Track. This decision will then be shown next to the course choice. ■

UNDERSTANDING THE RESPONSES

"The emails from UCAS Track, which just tell you 'something has changed' are very vague until you log onto the site itself. I also found it confusing working out the exact conditions of offers. You have to look at your cover letter, but then also at the actual offer you have been given."

Tash, French and Spanish student at UCL

Ingram Publishing/Thinkstock

WHAT CAN YOU EXPECT AT INTERVIEW?

Most applicants will not be called for interview, but if they are, then they should view it as a chance to shine.

Very few universities interview applicants these days, largely because of the costs and logistics involved. Most will make offers based on the information in the UCAS form: Personal Statement, school reference, predicted grades and academic record. Nevertheless, some applicants can expect to be interviewed and if your child is one of them they should familiarise themselves with the likely format.

The interview is only one part of the assessment process and your child should not be too worried about it. Plenty of university applicants have had what they considered to be disastrous interviews but have still been offered a place on the basis of the accumulated evidence of their academic quality.

> Interviewers want your child to be themselves

University interviewers are not out to intimidate and frighten applicants and they are aware of the need for reassurance and sensitivity in what can be a nerve-wracking experience. In fact many students come out of the interview feeling it could have been more rigorous and demanding, such are the efforts made to put them at ease. Interviewers want your child to be themselves, and to allow them to demonstrate their skills and abilities. Universities also stress that they make their decisions based ▶

Oxford University Images/Rob Judges Photography

Oxford and Cambridge rarely offer places without an interview, or series of interviews. Cambridge interviews around 80% of applicants, Oxford around two-thirds. At Cambridge, the interviews are usually completed in one day; at Oxford the process can last up to three days, with accommodation provided. UCL and Imperial College London also interview a large number of students.

on academic ability and potential, not on etiquette, appearance or background.

However, it is important that your child has the chance to present themselves in the most effective way in an interview, the purpose of which is to assess your child's academic ability and, most importantly, potential. Interviewers want to see if candidates can think on their feet and use their knowledge in original ways, as well as discover if they will be rewarding to teach. They will also be evaluating your child's commitment to the course, so they should ensure they can articulately explain why they wish to study their chosen subject at that institution.

Group interviews

Many departments invite applicants for a seminar-type small group interview. These are primarily concerned with giving information about the department, rather than assessing the student, though intelligent—but not too pushy—participation might impress academic staff.

amana productions inc/THINKSTOCK

THE INSIDE TRACK

"The interview begins when you get stuck."
OXFORD TUTOR

Testing aptitude, not knowledge

Remember that the interview is more about how you think than what you know. Knowledge is essential—every comment has to be supported by evidence—but more important is the ability to think with clarity, relevance, logic and originality. Don't shy away from straying into unfamiliar areas. There is nothing wrong with having a go, after admitting that this is something which is new to you. It is your imaginative and thoughtful response to the awkward question which could well clinch a place.

All interviews are different. Your child will almost certainly come ▶

AUTHOR'S TIPS

10 TIPS TO PASS ON TO YOUR CHILD

1 **It is said that the impression made in the first two minutes is what counts most. As you go in, stand upright, throw your shoulders back and at least feel and look as though you are confident.**

2 If it is appropriate, shake hands with interviewers and address them by name.

3 Look at the interviewer, make eye contact and try to smile from time to time.

4 **Don't sit in too relaxed a manner—sitting upright without crossing your legs and leaning slightly forward can give a good impression.**

5 If you don't know what to do with your hands, keep them clasped in your lap—but gestures can imply enthusiasm.

6 Try to relax and enjoy the interview—what better than to have time just to talk about yourself and the subject you are passionate about! Above all, just be yourself; it is you as an individual they want to know about.

7 **Support everything you say with evidence.**

8 Take time to think before answering and ask for guidance if you are having a real problem. Answer questions fully but don't waffle. Remember that there may not be a 'correct' answer; it is your thinking which is important.

9 Make sure you are answering the question the interviewer has asked, and not the one for which you have prepared.

10 **Don't be afraid to change your mind if the interviewer provides new information about a topic.**

shironosov/iStock/THINKSTOCK

psphotograph/iStock/THINKSTOCK

THE INSIDE TRACK

"Among other things, interviews are a good time to assess an applicant's ability to communicate and to cope with stress."
BRISTOL UNIVERSITY

out saying 'That was not at all what I was expecting'—though effective preparation will give them the confidence and intellectual flexibility to cope with any eventuality and present themselves well. Remember too that, if your child found the interview hard, that can be a good omen: the interviewers will have been pushing to the limits to see if your child will cope with a demanding course.

What will they ask?

Contrary to what many people think, most interview questions are straightforward and rarely do interviewers pose 'trick' questions. Applicants will often be asked pretty obvious questions; what is important is the quality of the answer. That said, the interview is meant to push candidates to their intellectual limits and questions may well be demanding and searching. Questions will almost all be designed in such a way as to allow for follow up questions and further discussion. Remember that the interview is designed to test how you think, not just what you know. It is also designed to see if your child is the sort of person who is right for that particular course at that university. ■

Applicants for vocational and practical courses are more likely to have an interview than those applying for humanities or social sciences. Most successful applicants for Medicine, Dentistry and Veterinary Medicine/Science will have to be interviewed first—as will applicants for special scholarships or awards.

Those wanting to study Drama, Theatre Studies and Music will probably have to attend auditions as part of the application process. The same may be true of applicants for Sports Science. Applicants for courses linked to art and design will often have an interview involving the presentation of a portfolio of work.

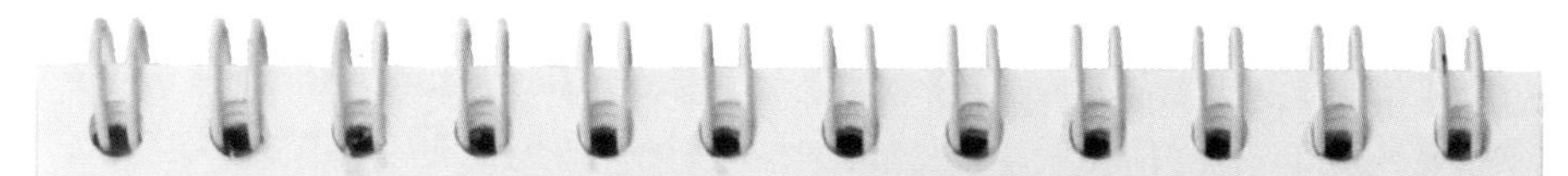

10 questions interviewers might ask

1. *Which aspects of this subject interest you—and why?*
2. *In your Personal Statement, you mentioned that you have enjoyed reading X. Can you summarise the conclusions of this book? Do you agree with them?*
3. *What have you learned about your subject from the work experience you mentioned in your Personal Statement?*
4. *What are the qualities needed to be a successful student of subject X?*
5. *You are a good sports player / musician / actor. Won't this be a distraction from studying?*
6. *Will your non-academic interests help you become a good student of subject X?*
7. *Talk about an aspect of subject X which has been in the news recently and which interests you.*
8. *What has been the most important development in subject X over the past fifty years?*
9. *We have 20 applicants for every place to study subject X. Why should we take you?*
10. *What do you think your Head and teachers have said about you in their reference?*

WHAT KIND OF INTERVIEW PREPARATION IS NEEDED?

The simple answer to this is not too much. It's important for your child's confidence that they make some preparation, but it's more important that they're ready for anything.

The starting point for interview preparation is to make sure your child has the opportunity to discuss their chosen subject in a broad context which goes beyond the confines of the sixth form syllabus. Schools will often provide subject-specific extension groups and recommended reading to ensure your child is aware of new ideas and novel ways of considering topics which they should then be prepared to discuss: the ability to challenge conventional wisdom is something which universities value hugely. You can help by having discussions at home and encouraging your child to be aware of unconventional opinions and approaches. University websites all have plenty of sensible, full guidance about interviews and interview preparation.

As far as specific training for an interview is concerned, it is important not to be over-prepared, either in terms of manner or academic content. Your child needs to behave as they would normally and to be themselves, while the biggest mistake many interviewees make is to talk about the material they have prepared rather than answer the question posed by the interviewer.

It is also advisable for your child to ask to see a copy of the school reference submitted with their UCAS application whilst they are preparing for interview. Their teachers may have referred to particular areas of their academic interest or books they believe they have read so it will be helpful to see what has been included to ensure they can address any related questions that may come up. In fact, when the interview forms a central element of the application process, it would be sensible for your child to ask to check any specific information included regarding achievements and reading to ensure it is correct before the reference is added to their UCAS form. Your ▶

10 WAYS TO PREPARE FOR AN INTERVIEW

1 **Find out what to expect. How many people will be interviewing you? Do you need to bring anything? Will the interview involve an activity?**

2 Re-read your **Personal Statement** and any material you have submitted: these may provide the basis of the interview.

3 Read over your A level or IB **subject notes**: you may be asked which topic you have enjoyed most and why, and all your answers need to be supported by knowledge-based evidence.

4 **Read a quality newspaper and magazine related to your subject: interviewers may ask for your opinions on current affairs or recent developments in your field.**

5 Make sure you can talk about some **new aspects** of your chosen subject which are not in the A level/IB syllabus or on your UCAS form.

6 Talk to your school's university advisor to see if they have any **feedback** from former students who have been interviewed at the same university.

7 Think of some **questions** to ask. How is the course assessed? What teaching methods are used? However, make sure they're not already answered in the prospectus or on the website.

8 **Have a mock interview or two, ideally with teachers or colleagues of your parents who do not know you too well.**

9 Think about **what to wear**. Dress smartly but comfortably: you may have a long day ahead of you.

10 **Have a good night's sleep beforehand.**

child's school may have a particular policy with regard to showing references before they are submitted so it will be important to make it clear that this is purely to ensure the information is accurate, as they could be questioned on anything included in the reference.

Practising at home

The school should organise interview training and opportunities for a mock interview; teachers will have the subject knowledge to quiz your child rigorously as well as an understanding of what universities will be looking for. Some schools swap interview candidates to give them an experience of unfamiliar faces and surroundings. However, any added practice which your child can get at home is only to be welcomed—though it is probably best if it is undertaken in a fairly light-hearted way. It will be more productive if your child is aware of some of the tips already indicated.

There is no reason why members of the family or family friends should not make up an interviewing panel: they can be briefed about the sort of questions likely to be asked. Perhaps you could all sit behind a table and your child will have to behave as if at the real thing: waiting outside the room, coming in, greeting people,

THE INSIDE TRACK

"Applicants should be ready to answer questions about why they applied to the university, why that subject, and why they are well-suited to the course—as well as their motivation, interests, future career plans, and any projects the applicant is very proud of having done."

SOUTHAMPTON UNIVERSITY

f-use/THINKSTOCK

sitting appropriately and then responding to your questions.

Afterwards, do not feel you have to provide critical feedback, though it will be good to emphasise positive points. It is much better simply to ask your child how they felt it went and whether they feel there are ways in which their performance could be improved. Try to avoid latching on to those idiosyncrasies which annoy you; the actual interviewer may be oblivious to them.

HERE TO HELP

"Don't panic. Interviews are an opportunity to show your calibre as a future undergraduate. A practice interview with your school or an education company such as Enjoy Education will increase your confidence and clarify your thinking."

VIVIENNE DURHAM, FORMER HEAD OF A LONDON SCHOOL

Critical thinking and open-mindedness

As part of your child's interview, they may be given a general exercise to test their powers of argument, analysis and understanding and ability to assimilate and express new ideas. The best way to prepare for this is simply to practise; Critical Thinking exercises such as those outlined in The Parent Brief's *Aiming Higher* can help in the dissection of arguments.

Your child could, for example, be given a short newspaper article and asked to summarise and comment on it; this could be on something in the news or about a more general issue.

Alternatively, they could be given an exercise in outlining the arguments for and against a controversial issue, such as capital punishment, euthanasia, legalising 'soft drugs', or giving prisoners the vote. ■

"We had a month's notice for my daughter's History of Art interview at Cambridge, and so we visited loads of art exhibitions. My other daughter only had about four days' notice from Oxford—but luckily the school had given her lots of interview preparation. Throughout the whole process we found the schools extremely helpful."

KATE, MOTHER OF TWO DAUGHTERS NOW AT UNIVERSITY AND A 15-YEAR-OLD SON

Comstock/Stockbyte/THINKSTOCK

WHAT DECISION DO WE HAVE TO MAKE NEXT?

Once all the offers are in, it's time to start narrowing down your options.

There are three choices that may be made at this stage: which course to accept as the Firm choice, which course to accept as the Insurance choice, and which course(s) to decline. Your child must reply to their offers at the same time.

Firm choice

A Firm acceptance means that this course is their first choice. Your child is making a commitment to attend the university, provided any additional conditions (such as exam results) are met.

The decision is therefore a very important one and should be considered carefully before replying.

Insurance choice

If the Firm acceptance relates to a conditional offer, your child should also choose an Insurance choice as a backup. This means that if the place at their Firm choice is not confirmed (because they do not fulfil the conditions), they have the opportunity to be accepted elsewhere.

For an Insurance acceptance to act as an effective backup, the conditions should be lower than the Firm acceptance. Even if your son or daughter does not have an effective backup, i.e. the remaining offers they have require conditions higher than their Firm or first choice, it is still sensible to select a course as their Insurance choice because universities will sometimes be flexible with grade conditions when results are released.

Replying to offers

Once your child has selected their Firm and Insurance choices, they will need to reply to their offers in UCAS Track before the reply date. The reply date is displayed in Track once your child has received decisions from all their university choices.

Before formally replying, your child should be certain that their Firm choice is their first choice university, and that they would be prepared to attend their Insurance choice university should they not meet the conditions of their Firm choice.

They can change their replies once within 14 days of initially replying but they will need to call UCAS (with their Personal ID) to do so. However, it is preferable to make their final decision before replying by the deadline. ■

WHAT IF MY CHILD DOESN'T GET AN OFFER?

It's unusual for a candidate to receive no offers, but if your child is in this unfortunate position there's still a chance they can go to university.

If your son or daughter has not yet used all their five choices, they can add more when Extra opens in February up until the beginning of July. If they have used all five choices, and have not received any offers (or have decided to decline all offers they have received), then they will also be able to use UCAS Extra.

UCAS Extra

Extra is open between late February and early July. Applicants will be able to see if they are eligible for Extra as it will show as a button when they log in to UCAS Track.

A list of courses with places available in Extra will be available using the UCAS Course Search facility. Only one course at a time can be added; there is no limit to the number of times an additional choice can be added within the designated period but only one choice can be considered at a time. As a result, if your child receives an offer which they are happy to accept they will not have an Insurance choice.

When a choice is added in Extra, UCAS submits your child's existing application to the university. If your child decides to apply for a different course, it is best to contact the university and ask if a replacement Personal Statement can be submitted relevant to the new course choice.

Universities have 21 days to make a decision once a choice is added in Extra. If your child receives an offer they wish to accept, they will need to accept this in UCAS Track. They cannot then apply to any further courses in Extra. If your child decides to decline an offer or a decision is not received within 21 days they may add another choice.

If your child does not receive an offer through Extra which they wish to accept, they can use Clearing to try and find an alternative place.

Your child may also consider applying to one of the UK's independent universities; the New College of the Humanities, for example, has a rolling online application system with no deadlines. ■

Parenting

nemphotography/iStock/THINKSTOCK

Having completed the process of application your child will inevitably be disheartened if they receive rejections, particularly if they have set their heart on a particular course or university. They will only feel worse if their friends are getting offers. Rejection from Oxford or Cambridge can be particularly hard, especially if your child had the excitement of being called for interview. As a parent, it is obviously your role to support and comfort your child through what will, to them, seem a very personal sense of rejection. Take their disappointment seriously; this may be the first major failure in their lives.

GET MOTIVATED

Rejections can have a serious effect on motivation: what is the point of working hard if I don't have any offers? This is where it is crucial to move forward by applying through Extra, talking about Adjustment (see p. 90) and reapplication after results and in general reinforcing the message that, the better the sixth-form qualifications, the better your child's chance of eventually getting the course and university they want.

ASK YOURSELF...

Am I letting my own disappointment show?

BE PREPARED

Early in the application stage, before too much work or emotion has been invested, it is worth discussing the eventuality of rejections by all five choices and to come up with an alternative plan of action: using Extra, deferring application for a year, taking a gap year, entering the world of work etc. The issue has then at least been confronted and there is an agreed way forward. Adolescent pain can quickly evaporate once there is something new on which to focus.

ASK YOUR CHILD...

Would you be genuinely happy if you had to go to your insurance-offer university?

You have only got one offer. Is this really where you want to go? We can always find other options.

WHAT HAPPENS ON RESULTS DAY?

Results day can bring surprises or disappointments. It is wise to be prepared for all eventualities.

The UCAS system is geared to the date when A level and Pre-U results are published on the third Thursday in August. If your child has taken IB exams, they will have their results early in July, but if they have missed their offers they may have to wait until mid-August for universities to make decisions.

If at all possible, your child should be in the UK when results come out. This makes contact with schools and universities much more straightforward; trying to manage complexities from overseas can be a nightmare.

Ideally, both you and your child would be at home on results day with reliable phone and Internet connection in ▶

> "Results day was stressful for us as my daughter had just missed her offer. Cambridge took 24 hours to confirm her place, which was made worse as we were in Hawaii and 11 hours behind the UK. I definitely advise parents to stay in the country!"
>
> **KATE,** MOTHER OF TWO DAUGHTERS AT UNIVERSITY AND A 15-YEAR-OLD SON

Nick White/Digital Vision/THINKSTOCK

order to contact universities. The phone lines will be busy so parents can help call; however the university will expect to speak with your child.

Getting exam results

Schools will have received your child's results 24 hours before the official publication date, and so will have had a day to prepare whatever means of notification is used. Note that the school cannot disclose results before the official publication day.

Many schools still ask students to come into school to receive their results on paper, partly so that individuals who need support receive it. Boarding schools generally telephone students with their results (encourage your teenager to delay discussion of the results until later in the day, as others will be waiting desperately to hear how they did), but emails are being used increasingly. Make sure your child knows what system their school is using, and sticks to the guidelines (eg wait for someone to phone you rather than phoning the school).

UCAS and universities get the results first, and so their decision may appear in Track from first thing on results day. Keep checking the UCAS website for confirmation which is not always immediate.

Last-minute decisions

If your child has changed their mind about taking up a first choice place, then they must contact the university at the earliest opportunity to be released from what is in effect a contract. If they are doing this to opt for their Insurance offer they must check that this university is happy to have them. This situation can get quite complex; contact all those involved as soon as possible. If they are going to reapply for the following year, UCAS should be informed once the rejected university has been contacted. If your child wants to defer their place they must also contact the university concerned.

Close calls

Candidates who have narrowly missed the grades they need may still be offered places at their Firm or Insurance choices. Keep in touch with UCAS or contact the university directly to see what is happening. Make sure that UCAS knows of any changes in contact details; this can be crucial at this stage.

If your child has missed the grade conditions for either their Firm and/or Insurance, they may be offered a place on an alternative course ('changed course offer'), which they will need to accept or decline.

Understanding IB results

If your child has gained the required number of points for their first choice then their place is guaranteed.

If your child has just missed the points requirement, it is well worth getting in touch with the university concerned. They may confirm a place immediately, aware that a point or two at IB is different from being a grade or two below an A level offer. Alternatively, they may suggest waiting until A level results are out and possibly offer a place then.

On or shortly after A level results day, your child's chosen universities should have made their final decision which will appear in Track. Clearing will then be open. ■

A STUDENT SPEAKS

RESULTS SUCCESS

"I checked UCAS Track first thing on the morning of results day and saw that I had been accepted to my first choice university. It was another few hours before I got the phone call with my exam results—but at that point, we were already celebrating the good news!"

Emma, English Literature graduate from Newcastle

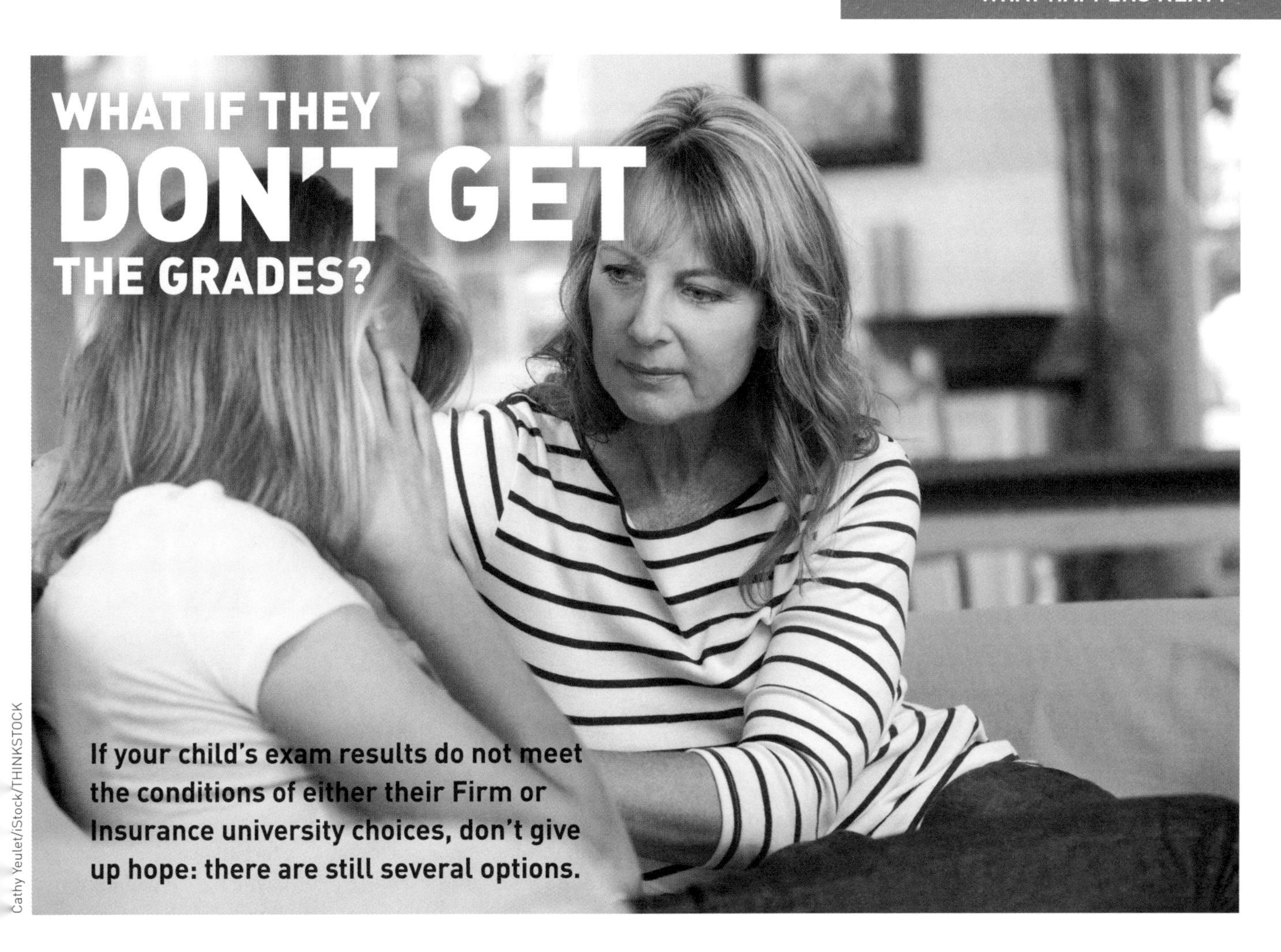

WHAT IF THEY DON'T GET THE GRADES?

If your child's exam results do not meet the conditions of either their Firm or Insurance university choices, don't give up hope: there are still several options.

Applicants who do not meet the conditions of their offers might be offered a place on an alternative course by either their first choice or insurance choice universities. This course will usually be related to the course originally applied for: for example, an applicant for History who has not quite made the grade may be offered a place on an Economic History or European Studies course.

Re-marks

Students may want to have one or more of their papers re-marked, particularly if they are only a few marks under a grade threshold and this has resulted in their losing a university place. But remember, marks can go down as well as up. Don't go for a re-mark if you are close to the lower grade boundary: your overall grade might go down. And if you have got your desired place, don't risk a re-mark for the sake of pride! Take advice from your teachers as to whether a re-mark is advisable and get them to fast track the process. It is possible to get back a copy of the relevant paper before deciding on a re-mark, but you do not want to miss the 31st August deadline set by most universities for holding places pending re-marks.

If your child is going for a re-mark, it is essential they tell the university at which they have narrowly missed a place and ask them to hold the place pending the outcome. They should keep your place open until 31st August, but are not obliged to do so. If as a result of a re-mark you achieve the grades to satisfy your offer, you may instead be offered a deferred place for the following year. Tell the university when the re-mark comes through.

Alternatively, your child may decide to reapply next year—possibly resitting some exams —or they may now consider options other than university (**see p. 108**). They will also be eligible to look for a university place in Clearing. This will be indicated in UCAS Track.

Clearing

Clearing is an excellent opportunity for applicants who have not been accepted by their chosen universities to secure a place on another course. While your ▶

shironosov/iStock/THINKSTOCK

> Clearing opens in July but full vacancy lists are not published until A level results day; it closes for applications approximately a month later. Clearing can also be used by those who did not apply through UCAS by 30 June.

AUTHOR'S TIPS

4 SOURCES OF HELP FOR YOU AND YOUR CHILD

1 Staff at your child's school know their academic profile, so this should be your first port of call for advice and support.

2 The **UCAS Clearing system** is easy to use and provides all the information your child needs about alternative courses. It can make sense to select some courses from Clearing and then phone the universities concerned.

3 Universities are keen to fill places as soon as possible and have teams of trained advisers to help sort out problems and speed things up. Your child should try to get through to a specific department as early as possible on results day, but be patient if they are held in a queue. Many phone-callers are quite fraught, so politeness and thanks may well enhance the chances of success!

4 Newspaper supplements published the weekend after results day are usually full of advice, information and advertisements from academic institutions wanting to recruit students.

child may be extremely upset and disappointed at this time (as they have not fulfilled the conditions for either their Firm or Insurance choices) it is important that they remain calm and focused and in the right frame of mind to contact universities and work hard to secure a place.

Every year there are university (including Russell Group) places available on competitive courses but these are limited so it is essential your child responds quickly, contacting the universities as early as possible and in their order of preference. It is, therefore, advisable that they have already considered which courses they would be willing to accept should they be offered a place, and have made a list of these with the relevant contact numbers for Clearing. These are available on the university websites.

When they get through to the university, your child should explain their situation, what their results are and why they wish to apply for a place on the course. It is also helpful to have considered why they believe they will be a committed undergraduate and likely to succeed on the course. For some courses, your child may be connected with a lecturer to have an informal discussion about the course. The Admissions tutors will advise your child about their options and what to do next if an offer is made. Although Clearing does require you and your child to act quickly, it is essential to take the time

monkeybusinessimages/iStock/THINKSTOCK

necessary to make an informed choice.

Your child can contact as many universities as they wish. They should try and secure offers over the telephone and then take time to decide which one to accept. Once they have made their choice, they should add their Clearing choice in Track; it is important to add a Clearing choice only once they have had confirmation of a place from the university. To add a choice, click 'Add Clearing choice' and complete the course details by the date the university indicated on the telephone. This represents your child formally accepting the offer, so when the university confirms, it will show as an acceptance on the choices page of UCAS Track and they will be sent a confirmation letter. Only one choice can be added at a time; if the university does not confirm the place, it will be possible to add another choice.

It may also be necessary to visit universities at short notice if your child is not familiar with a university who makes them an offer through Clearing. ■

RESULTS SUCCESS

"I found Clearing quite stressful because of my circumstances. I missed the grades to get into Manchester, but because I had interviewed there in Spanish and so they knew my ability, they tried their best to get me on the course regardless. While I was waiting they weren't prepared to release me into Clearing, so I felt like a ticking time bomb literally watching university places slip away. In the end Manchester weren't able to offer me my place, and by this time very few courses were left. Luckily I got an offer from Coventry the very next day. It all worked out so well in the end but the process was a bit muddled in between."

Rachel, French and Spanish graduate from Coventry University

LWA/Dann Tardif/Blend Images/THINKSTOCK

WHAT IF MY CHILD DOES BETTER THAN EXPECTED?

If your child gets a pleasant surprise on results day they can take advantage of the UCAS Adjustment facility and 'trade up' to a different course or university.

When exam results are released your child may find they have achieved grades better than those required to fulfil the conditions of their Firm choice. If this is the case they will be eligible to use UCAS Adjustment to look for a university place they would prefer.

Adjustment is available from mid-August to the end of August and is open only to applicants who have met and exceeded the terms of their Firm choice. Your child will not be eligible to use Adjustment if they have missed their first choice but exceeded the grades required for their Insurance choice.

Your child can register for Adjustment through UCAS Track. Once registered, applicants have five days to secure a place (specifically, five 24-hour periods starting from the moment of registration).

Applicants need to act quickly to approach their preferred universities; it is important to advise them that the approach is coming through Adjustment, not Clearing. Applicants can contact as many universities as they like.

To accept an offer in Adjustment, the university should be advised and they will update Track to confirm acceptance. If no place is found, your son or daughter will go to their Firm choice university.

Planning ahead

If your child comes out of their exams thinking that they may have performed better than expected, it is sensible for them to have considered in advance which universities/courses they would be keen to approach to ask if a place were available. ■

AVAVA/iStock/THINKSTOCK

IS IT POSSIBLE TO REAPPLY?

If your child has a change of heart, they may wish to start UCAS entirely from scratch.

After receiving their results, your child may decide to withdraw their application and reapply for the following year. There are various reasons for doing this: they may have had a change of heart about the subject(s) they want to study or the university they want to attend; they may have decided to take a gap year, but their chosen universities will not defer their place; they may feel that they need more practical experience before embarking on a vocational course; or they may have done better or worse than expected in their exams but not achieved the desired result through Adjustment (**see p. 90**) or Clearing (**see p. 87**).

In these cases, reapplying can be the right strategy, and is certainly much better than embarking on a course half-heartedly and adding to the student dropout numbers (over 32,000 in the academic year 2012–13). If your child already has their grades it makes choosing appropriate courses and universities far less of a lottery and universities are likely to respond quickly to the application. ■

THE INSIDE TRACK

"The most successful reapplications are those which offer some sense of advancement or development from the original application. Students shouldn't worry about reapplying to universities they've previously declined offers from: anyone can change their minds!"

SHEFFIELD UNIVERSITY

If your teenager already has a place, they will need to check that the university will release them to reapply.

AUTHOR'S TIPS

6 THINGS TO REMEMBER

1. Your child will need to write a **new Personal Statement:** they will have more up-to-date information to include, and universities may expect a post-results applicant to be more mature.

2. Your child's school will need to provide an **updated reference**.

3. University offers vary from year to year; your child will need to re-do their **research**.

4. Applying with the **support network** of a school can make things easier; if possible your child should go into their old school to liaise with university advisers and teachers.

5. Universities will expect your child to **use the year productively** in gaining work experience or furthering their studies.

6. Some universities have policies about the grades achieved at a re-sit: it is generally thought that it is **more difficult** to get an offer for a place on a competitive course if you are re-sitting, and some universities will not accept re-sit results. That said, many universities accept that re-sitting is a sign of motivation. Your child should contact universities to see what their attitude is.

Parenting

The keys to dealing with this potentially stressful period of anticipation and possible disappointment are support, understanding and practicality. It is important that your child knows that your concern for them is not conditional on exam results—and too many parents fail to make it clear that, whatever the outcome, they will still support their child.

Milenko Bokan/iStock/TH-INKSTOCK

ASK YOUR CHILD...

Before you look into Adjustment, are you sure you're not perfectly happy with your current first choice?

WHAT YOUR CHILD MIGHT BE WORRYING ABOUT

- Have I made the right choices?
- How will I face my parents and friends if I don't get the necessary grades?
- How will my parents react if I change my mind?
- The whole application process has been hard work. Do I want to go through it again?

PREPARE YOURSELF

It will be easier to support your child through disappointments if you have pre-empted your response to the various outcomes: if your child has not performed as well as they hoped, what they will need is support, comfort, practical advice and a positive view of the future.

STEP BACK

While you may be tempted to make phone calls to universities yourself, it is your child who should do the talking. They are more likely to be convincing than you are!

MAKE SURE THEY'RE HAPPY

Whether they have got their first choice, their insurance offer or gained a place through Clearing, be alert if your child seems uneasy at the outcome. It may be natural nervousness at starting a new stage in their life, but if they are genuinely having misgivings about the course or university for which they have been accepted, this is the time to talk about reapplying and other options. Deciding to reapply can reduce tensions and leave time for a measured and sensible reappraisal of your child's future.

ASK YOURSELF...

Are you sure your child is going to the university they want for the course they want, not the one you want?

Fuse/THINKSTOCK

WHAT WILL UNIVERSITY BE LIKE?

Is your child ready for the responsibilities and practicalities of university life?

After the stress of the application process and exams, there can a palpable sense of relief when your child actually has a place at the university they want to attend for a subject they want to study. So much so, indeed, that it is easy to forget about the practicalities of the large step they are about to take. Within a short time your offspring is going to be an independent adult (well, semi-independent), on their own for much of the year and potentially immune from the guidance you feel you can give. Some preparation for life away from home and school is therefore essential if your child is to make the most of life at university—and the first few weeks can make all the difference to their experience. ■

A STUDENT SPEAKS

HOW UNIVERSITY IS DIFFERENT FROM SCHOOL

"At school you study to someone else's schedule; at university you study to your own. I enjoyed the luxury of managing my own time (something you often don't get even in the workplace) but I noticed a lot of people struggled, especially in first year, to realise that if no-one was chasing them up it didn't mean that they didn't have to do the work."

Antonia, History graduate from Durham

AUTHOR'S TIPS

6 CHALLENGES AT UNIVERSITY

1 University courses require a lot of **independent learning**: students are expected to undertake most work on their own initiative.

2 **A student's work may be given minimal feedback. This can be hard for students accustomed to being motivated by close attention or praise from teachers.**

3 The majority of a student's time is unstructured and it is essential that your child quickly learns **time management**.

4 **The teaching style is very different from school: on some courses the smallest teaching group may be a seminar of 20 and there's no obligation to contribute.**

5 At university, there are so many **distractions** (societies, sport, social activities, music, drama etc) and these can be much more attractive and exciting than studying. Important as it is to take full advantage of everything a university has to offer, your child must be disciplined: academic work comes first.

6 Some students need time to adjust to **greater intellectual demands** and originality of outlook demanded at university.

WHERE WILL MY TEENAGER LIVE?

A secure base is vital for well-being, especially in the first year.

When considering universities it is sensible to discuss the practicalities of life at each of those your child is considering. Even though it may not be the final determining factor, they should be aware if there is going to be a half-hour bus ride each day to get to lectures, whether they will be able to get back to their room during the day and how far they will be from shops, the city centre, clubs or the university sports facilities—whatever is important to them.

University accommodation options and the costs involved are presented in detail on university websites—though remember that universities are keen to sell themselves through the apparent attractiveness of their facilities. If finance is an issue it is crucial to investigate the price variables between different universities and options at the same university. Depending on the town or city and the institution concerned, your child could be paying less than £100 a week (the lowest student rents are apparently in Northern Ireland) to getting on for £300 in London.

Most universities offer accommodation to all first year students and many can provide somewhere to live for two years, if not the full length of the course. In general the older universities have more purpose-built accommodation under their direct control; there is likely to be less available at the former polytechnics and colleges which became universities in the 1990s and afterwards.

Each university has its own system for allocating accommodation. Once your child has firmly accepted an offer, they should immediately look at the website of the university concerned to discover how to apply for accommodation. In many cases, they can do this the moment they have firmly accepted an offer, though some universities only begin the process at a later point, say in the March before a student is going to university. If it is at

SimonKR/iStock/THINKSTOCK

Rich Legg/iStock/THINKSTOCK

all possible, try to visit the university with your child to see for yourself the options available: this may provide a good reality check and reinforce the importance of making the right decision. If your child is applying for university accommodation they will almost certainly be given some initial choice—but the university will then have a system for allocating places in the event of demand outstripping supply. Once your child's university place is confirmed the accommodation will also be confirmed and you may well be asked for a deposit to secure it, often to be submitted in a matter of days. Those who have received places through Clearing or Adjustment may have to take what they are offered as more popular options may all have been taken. ▶

THIS MAY HELP

There is a great diversity of provision among universities in the type, quality and cost of accommodation available, and the Which University online guide has some excellent advice.

James Woodson/DigitalVision/THINKSTOCK

University halls of residence

This is the most popular option for first year students and one provided by almost all universities. The halls may be close to the teaching facilities on campus universities such as Warwick, Lancaster and Kent or some distance away from the main university—often the case in red-brick, metropolitan universities such as Manchester, Southampton or Liverpool. Some halls are vast, with over 1,000 students and their own small shopping malls; others may just be for a few hundred. There is still single-sex accommodation in some universities, particularly for women. Most of the accommodation consists of single bedsits, though there may be some shared rooms (with a reduced price) or one-bedroomed flats (at a higher cost). The buildings have 24-hour access and generally boast good security systems. Halls will nearly always have social facilities, including the all-important student bar, washing machines and common rooms. Facilities may also be limited if the Student Union is nearby.

Some universities (eg Durham, Kent, York) have a version of the collegiate system. A student's hall of residence is their 'college' and, at Durham at least, colleges do have distinctive qualities.

Privately managed halls of residence

These work in exactly the same way as the university-run halls, except that they are owned by private companies who work in co-operation with the university. As commercial concerns, their standards—and rents—may be higher, but not always.

Private rented accommodation

Many students, particularly after their first year, like the idea of sharing their own place with friends. Almost all universities have accommodation offices with a register of private landlords who are subjected to stringent inspection procedures. There is nothing to stop your child simply renting property through a commercial agent or answering an advertisement—but organising a tenancy through the university provides an element of greater protection. Rents can be exorbitant, especially in London, Oxford or Cambridge, in towns and

"If your child needs you to be a guarantor for their rent, be careful that you don't end up financially liable for any of their friends. Your child should take the same precautions and make sure bills are set up in everybody's name, not just one. My son lived with six other students and it took him eight months to get back another student's share of the electricity bill. In my daughter's house, they each signed up for one of the utilities and then worked out a way of making it fair."

ANGELA, PARENT OF THIRD YEAR STUDENT AND A RECENT GRADUATE

cities in areas with high property prices (eg Guildford or Brighton) or in smaller towns with large student populations (eg Durham or St Andrews). You may be required to act as surety, which gives you some financial leverage with uncooperative landlords.

Buying a house

Some parents buy a property in which their child can live along with friends; the rent could provide an income for their child. At the end of the university course the property can be let out again or sold, hopefully at a profit.

Living at home

The UK, unlike many countries, has developed a tradition of students going away from home to study. However, studying close to and living at home can make financial sense: your child will not have to pay rent and you can provide some of their meals. Not all universities will sanction this arrangement unless there are extenuating circumstances. ■

chrishowey/iStock/THINKSTOCK

9 THINGS TO **LOOK OUT FOR** IN THE SMALL PRINT

1. **What has to be paid, when and by what means? Is a deposit required?**

2. **What happens when a payment is late? Who is responsible: you or your child?**

3. What is provided as part of the deal? (Some halls of residence, for example, do not offer food at weekends or do not provide bedding.)

4. What is the length of the contract? (This is usually the academic year, 38–42 weeks.)

5. **Are there restrictions in using a room during vacations?**

6. What notice is required to end the contract and move out?

7. **What arrangements are there for security and supervision?**

8. What happens when things go wrong?

9. **What are the rules about overnight visitors?**

XiXinXing/THINKSTOCK

WHAT ESSENTIALS SHOULD STUDENTS TAKE?

Some parents drive their children to university, cars overflowing with home comforts from plants to soft toys. Other students arrive with barely a suitcase. What's actually necessary?

Before you buy anything, read the small print. You may remember travelling to university with a kettle, lamp and record player but these days all electrical appliances are required to be PAT tested so there may be rules about having these in student rooms. Don't spend huge amounts on domestic equipment: it is likely to get lost, purloined or damaged. Cheap hardware shops can provide all you need and IKEA also do good student starter-packs.

Once the domestic necessities are ticked off, think about the things that are essential for your child to feel comfortable and secure. This may be their own duvet and pillows (standard issue university bedding is fairly basic) or other small home comforts such as cushions or one or two family photos.

There is sometimes a gender divide here, with boys eschewing pretty much everything on offer (and then sheepishly asking for various items next time they come home). ■

THIS MAY HELP

If there is no room in the suitcase for cookery books, websites such as BBC Good Food have areas specially for students.

AUTHOR'S TIPS

10 ESSENTIALS TO BRING

1 **Bedding** (though check what is provided). Home bedding is likely to be of a higher standard.

2 Things with which to **personalise** a room (though look at the rules as to what can be put on the walls; Health and Safety and limited redecorating budgets might stifle your child's pretensions to interior design).

3 **Clothes hangers.**

4 **Kettle** (check regulations).

5 **Kitchen supplies**: mugs, plates, glasses and cutlery.

6 **Pots and pans**: a set of basic saucepans (a large one can double as an ovenproof casserole) and a baking tray.

7 **Kitchen utensils** (including a wooden spoon, tin opener and corkscrew).

8 One of the many **recipe books** for students on the market.

9 A first week survival box of **essential food supplies** eg. tea; coffee; cereals; biscuits; sweets; sugar; pasta; rice and some ready-made sauces; maybe some instant or easy-to-cook meals to tide them over the first week.

10 **A first aid kit.**

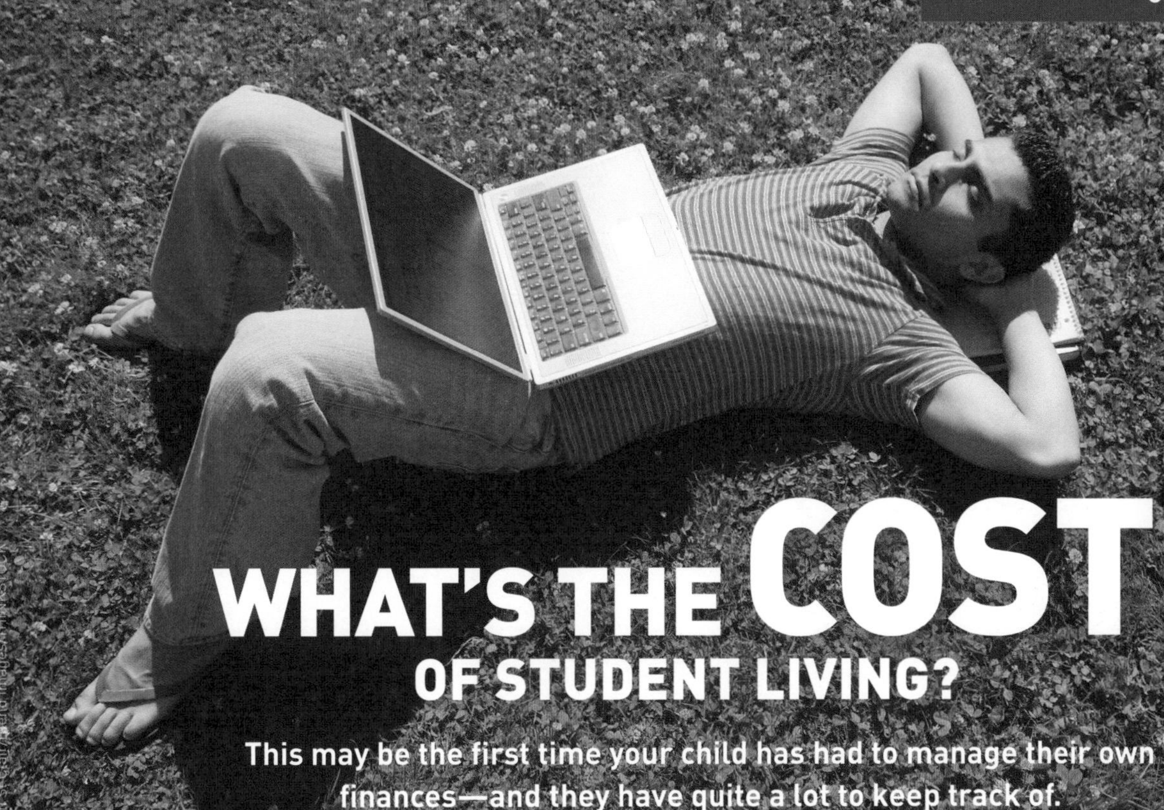

WHAT'S THE COST OF STUDENT LIVING?

This may be the first time your child has had to manage their own finances—and they have quite a lot to keep track of.

University does not come cheap. On top of tuition fees, your son or daughter will face the costs of accommodation, food and drink, books and stationery, a laptop, TV licence, insurance, society and union subscriptions, travel, and the costs of partaking in social activities!

Accommodation costs are often well in excess of £100 a week. Even with the most careful planning, food is likely to be at least £5 a day, more if students do not cater for themselves. One or two nightclub jaunts a week can quickly eat into any budget. ■

£15k to £20k a year is not an unreasonable estimate of the total sum involved—though some of this will be financed by a student loan, to be paid back once your child is in employment.

AUTHOR'S TIPS

8 WAYS TO HELP YOUR TEEN MANAGE THEIR FINANCES

1. **Work out a realistic budget and discuss where the money will be coming from.**

2. Establish what **you** are prepared to pay for and what you expect your child to finance.

3. Decide how **your contribution** will be paid to your child: a lump sum per term or monthly allowance, perhaps.

4. **Discuss major items of expenditure including travel (expensive, even with a student card).**

5. Banks are keen to attract students and there are plenty of enticing offers. Read the small print carefully and go for the **bank account** (and offer) which is best for your child.

6. **Make sure your child is aware of how credit and store cards work and the high rates of interest often charged.**

7. If money is likely to be tight your child may be considering a **part-time job**. Term time work could be a distraction from study and many universities discourage it; vacation work is preferable.

8. Discuss how to **budget and to organise finances** and what to do if there is a problem. Be prepared to bail your child out at least once (but don't advertise your willingness to do this).

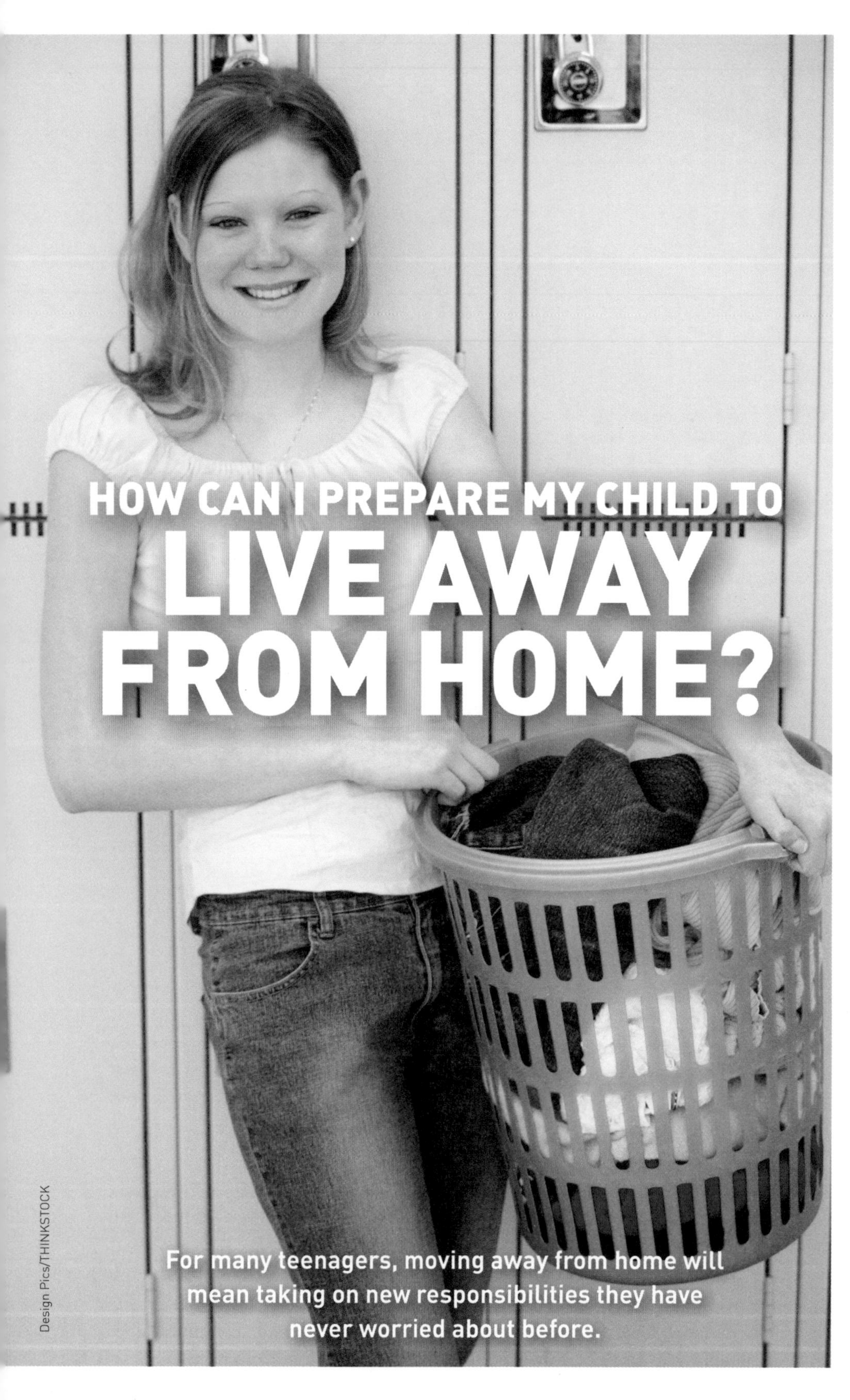

HOW CAN I PREPARE MY CHILD TO LIVE AWAY FROM HOME?

For many teenagers, moving away from home will mean taking on new responsibilities they have never worried about before.

Design Pics/THINKSTOCK

Being a student is about learning to be independent and about growing up—and this involves new experiences, experimentation and making mistakes. Unlike at home or even at school, your child will need to take responsibility for everything from looking after themselves when they are unwell to fixing problems around the house.

If possible, talk with your child about their new identity as a student in a new environment. Universities are wonderful microcosms of the real world: for the first time, your child may encounter people who are different from them in terms of social background, geographical origin, ethnicity, religious belief, sexual orientation, style, ability, appearance and outlook. Universities still espouse an atmosphere of liberal toleration and a delight in the celebration of difference—and your child will get the most out of their university experience if they embrace this outlook wholeheartedly, abandoning preconceptions and stereotypes and treating people as they are. You may wish to warn them that they may find they are stereotyped themselves because of the school they attended, or the area they grew up in—let alone the more worrying slurs linked to race, gender, appearance or sexual orientation. It is important to help them think of strategies by which they can be proud of themselves but also win over other people, break down stereotypical images and develop relationships with the widest possible cross-section of people.

Keeping healthy

Young people can be quite blase about diet and exercise. It might be worth having a friendly chat before they go off to university about the need to have a balanced, healthy diet, to get regular exercise and to develop sensible sleep patterns.

Your child can avoid the well documented phenomenon of Freshers' Flu by following normal hygiene (especially washing hands), pacing their activities and getting adequate amounts of sleep. However, as it is rather likely your child will not follow this advice during their first exciting week at university, give them a backup plan if they do get ill: remind them to register with a GP, and perhaps send them off with a first aid kit.

Universities often have their own medical centres with staff who are highly experienced in dealing with the whole range of medical issues students encounter in an utterly non-judgemental and sympathetic way.

Coping on their own

Life at university can be pressurised and your child may not be good at dealing with stress. Counselling can be an excellent way of combatting stress before it becomes a serious and debilitating issue: encourage your child to seek professional help if you feel they are not coping with life.

Universities often have professional counsellors to help students tackle problems and difficulties—and discussions are totally confidential. If you sense that your child is worried about something they will not discuss with you, encourage them to go and talk to one of the professionals who will give them the guidance, support and practical help they need, along with any medical advice or intervention which might be appropriate.

Steve Mason/Photodisc/THINKSTOCK

Drink, drugs and sex

You may also be worried about issues such as drink, drugs and sex. Your child will, of course, have had extensive health education at school—but there will always be a gap between what we know and what we do, and it is almost inevitable that, while at university, your child will get up to things you do not want to know about. It is worth having the (potentially embarrassing) conversation to make sure your child is approaching these things sensibly—as you will most likely not be able to dissuade them from partaking at all. ■

HOW WILL I COPE WITH SAYING GOODBYE?

A child's departure for university is tough for most parents. Some are taken aback by just how deeply they are affected but all agree that any sadness is relatively short-lived.

If you are taking your child to university—and most parents these days feel they ought to do this—help them move their belongings into their room, perhaps help them unpack and then go. Don't even think of staying around in the same town just to make sure they are settling in well. However worried you may be, it is now up to your child and the university to make things work—and your continued presence is unlikely to make things better. Simply trust them to cope: all those preparatory conversations and discussions will actually have had their effect.

It is likely that the worst time for you will be immediately after your child has gone to university. Not only are they no longer there physically, but you are also aware that this marks the start of their life as an adult. It is important that you do not have too much time to worry about what they are doing and whether they are coping.

Many mothers who have not worked while bringing up children feel this is the point to return to the workplace or at least involve themselves in a greater range of activities. Don't underestimate the sense of loss which fathers may also feel; they are still affected by the change in the family dynamic. Younger children can of course also occupy your time and this can be a good opportunity to devote more time and attention to them; the pressures of university application may have led them to feel a little neglected.

Will they change?

When your child comes home from university you will probably find them changed, but not that much. You will quickly realise that the family is still central to their life and that they continue to be dependent on you (and not just financially). However independent a student may seem, the offer to participate in an exciting family holiday, for example, is rarely resisted. ■

> "Even if you're feeling emotional at saying goodbye, don't let your child see this. Instead, let them sense your excitement at their new adventure; that is what will give them confidence—and it will make you feel happier too."
> **CAMILLA,** MOTHER OF TWO RECENT GRADUATES

monkeybusinessimages/iStock/THINKSTOCK

WHAT GOES ON IN THE FIRST FEW WEEKS?

University is such a formative experience that friends made during this time are likely to be people you will know for life.

It is sometimes said that students spend three years avoiding the 'friends' they made in their first week, and it is unlikely that your child will necessarily find their soulmate or lifelong buddy straightway. Encourage them to be outgoing and gregarious: suggest to your child that they are the one to offer coffee and cakes to their neighbours or to organise a trip into town, a local cheap restaurant, the union bar or a local pub. Knowing too many people is rarely a problem. You might also encourage your child to be welcoming towards the fellow student who is quiet or socially nervous, as well as being positively supportive of international students for whom the whole experience can be utterly bewildering.

Freshers' Week

Freshers' Week, or 'Welcome Week' as it's sometimes known, is held at the start of the academic year. In some places it could be up to two weeks of fun events and parties; in others, the 'week' is in fact three or four days of fun and then a quick reality check with the announcement of two essay deadlines and several reading lists. Orientation meetings introduce students to the campus, halls of residence, the academic departments and your library. Your child mustn't miss meetings with tutors and administration. Freshers' Week is a good chance to get to know the staff and lecturers as well, not just fellow students!

> Freshers' Week is about orientation to a new way of life

What to an outsider can seem like an orgy of hedonistic bacchanalian revelry is in fact a highly organised attempt by universities to make new students feel at home socially and academically and get them used to the idea of personal independence and life at university. Many universities invite freshers to come up a week before the other students so that orientation activities can start before term begins in earnest. ▶

Universities accept that Freshers' Week is about feeling at home and orientation to a new way of life: your child is unlikely to have many academic demands made of them. However, with short terms, students need to get down to work quickly: indeed the intensity of Freshers' Week can have a cathartic effect in draining the desire for further sociability. By the second week at university, they should be in the thick of study—and they should never forget that that is why they are there. This is where your child's self-discipline and organisational skills have to kick in. Attractive as all the clubs and societies at the Freshers' Fair may be, your child needs to rationalise their commitment and take time to decide where their true enthusiasms lie and how much time they have outside their academic programme. ■

IN THE KNOW

"Get involved in as much as possible. It's easier said than done, but getting involved in your students' union and in societies is a great way of meeting likeminded people. If you're living in halls, the people you're put with might not be your first choices as friends but it can be a great way to get to know someone that you wouldn't normally socialise with. Some of the most unlikely but wonderful friendships were formed in halls of residence.

And make sure your NUS Extra card is permanently in your wallet: the discounts make a real difference when you're on a budget!"

TAKEN FROM NUS (NATIONAL UNION OF STUDENTS) WEBSITE

Stockbyte/THINKSTOCK

A STUDENT SPEAKS

HOW TO BE RESPONSIBLE IN FRESHERS' WEEK

"The challenge of striking the balance between being as sociable as you can while also not crossing the line in doing so, whether it's by missing lectures, succumbing to peer pressure or blowing your budget in the first few weeks, makes me quite nervous. I just want to be careful not to get caught up in the whole 'fresher's life' and forget about the outside world and the other things which matter too, aside from my new environment and the pressures it brings."

Katie, applicant for Politics & International Relations

shironsov/iStock/THINKSTOCK

WHAT IF THEY'RE UNHAPPY?

Don't meet trouble half way but do be alert to the fact that for some young people the transition to university life is not straightforward.

If you sense that something is wrong, or your child admits that there are problems, resist the urge to race to their rescue; the last thing your child may want is for you to appear distraught on their doorstep. The fact that they are willing to talk and are not concealing their feelings is the first step to finding a solution. Allowing your child to talk, listening and expressing sympathy are obviously the best initial responses. For some problems there is immediate action your child can take, though solutions should come from them, not be imposed by you.

Support systems

There are plenty of people at the university on hand to help with worries: their tutor, the warden of their hall, a doctor or a university counsellor. If you continue to be worried, you can phone someone at the university—though they will not be able to disclose confidential details to you: universities are obliged to respect the privacy of students as adults in their own right. This may not be the right approach for emotional troubles but it is worth trying if your child's problem is concerned with, for instance, accommodation. A polite, but firm, word in the ear of the right person can resolve practical issues quickly.

And why not suggest your child comes home for a few days? It may be that all they need is a few days' rest and some parental coddling; it is also easier to talk face-to-face in a relaxed environment. This will give you the opportunity to explore things in greater depth, to listen and to think about strategies to deal with issues.

When to take it seriously

If dissatisfaction with the course and university is really deep-seated, it is possible that your child has made the wrong decision and needs time to rethink. If at the end of the first year it is clear that things are not right, then ▶

HERE TO HELP

"It may sound like a cliché, but encouraging a student to "give it time" is often useful. Many of the problems students experience at the beginning are a normal part of the transition to university life and do get better with time. For example, feelings of strangeness and dislocation, of not being known or feeling of little importance to others here, will ease as students gradually get to know other students and a few members of staff remember their names, and as they find some places on campus where they feel comfortable. Some people make friends more quickly than others."
NOTTINGHAM UNIVERSITY

your child should consider taking a year out and reapplying to other universities and for different subjects. There may be substantial financial penalties—but you may feel these are worth the eventual happiness of your child. If it is clear after a short time that your child is on the wrong course, the university may help with changing courses, but this will involve considerable work in catching up in the new subject while the right to change course is not automatic. Waiting to start again the following year might make better sense. ■

Jani Brysond/iStock/THINKSTOCK

AUTHOR'S TIPS

9 POTENTIAL **TRIGGERS FOR ANXIETY**

1. Your child may feel **disillusionment** with their course: the subject, the teaching or getting little or no feedback from teaching staff.
2. Academics have a habit of giving unsuspecting undergraduates long reading lists to master in a week or two with little guidance—leading to stress, self-doubt and **fear of failure.**
3. **They may feel a dissatisfaction with the university itself or the hall of residence.**
4. No matter how popular your child was at school, in a new environment, there's always a chance they'll have **difficulty making friends.**
5. **Relationships can cause anxiety, especially if a boyfriend/girlfriend is not at the same university.**
6. Students may face worries about **sexual issues**: pregnancy, birth control, STDs, orientation etc.
7. Students often feel rundown and exhausted as a result of a manic lifestyle: health issues such as ME and glandular fever are not uncommon.
8. **Financial worries can be particularly anxiety-inducing to a student newly taking on this responsibility.**
9. No longer is your child the big fish in a small pond they were at school: they may feel a general **lack of confidence.**

Parenting

There is simply so much to do at the start of your child's university career that they will have little time to miss you and their home; don't be upset if they are not as bereft as you are! Things may change a few weeks into term, when the all-consuming fun ends and the realities of life and work begin to impinge: that is when your continued support may be needed, particularly when your child is faced with difficult assignments or begins to doubt their innate ability. Sometimes, the start of the second term—in dismal January—produces a much more negative response, with none of the froth of Freshers' Week, compounded by post-Christmas and New Year blues.

Ingram Publishing/THINKSTOCK

SAY HELLO

Everybody likes to get post: why not send letters or exciting care parcels to cheer up a homesick student?

ASK YOURSELF...

Are you viewing your child as an independent adult?

KEEP IN TOUCH

With mobile phones, Skype and social media sites, keeping in touch should be no problem—but do not be too insistent and inquisitive. Your child will get in touch when they are ready and on their own terms and will almost certainly want to communicate their excitement at their new life—but don't expect them to tell you everything. If this is their first time living away from home, it can be unsettling—even at the age of 18 or 19—to have too much contact over the first days or weeks.

FIGHT SOME OF THEIR BATTLES

It is important you let your child take care of themselves, but there are certain battles they may still want you to fight. If, for example, when your child arrives at university, the accommodation is unsatisfactory, be prepared to kick up a fuss there and then. Students are not practised in complaining—but given the high rent often charged, they have a right to good facilities.

DON'T JUDGE

In their new independent life, your child may get up to things you're not necessarily happy about. No matter your opinion, however, tell them always to seek help if they need it. They need to know you will talk to them non-judgementally—or depending on your relationship, you may instead suggest a friend or family member to talk things through on your behalf.

AID/A.COLLECTIONRF/THINKSTOCK

WHAT ARE THE ALTERNATIVES TO UNIVERSITY?

University is not the right choice for everyone and there are many alternatives, which will enable your child to pursue a successful and fulfilling career.

After twelve or so years at school your son or daughter may require time to explore options and give further consideration to their future path before deciding which direction to take. Providing objective support and advice to them will be important as they contemplate their options.

Gap year

On leaving school, your child may not feel ready to commit to a university course for three or more years of study, or may not be clear about what they wish to study. A gap year **(see p. 22)** can be used in a variety of ways, including to gain skills and qualifications through work experience and short courses in an area/areas of interest and to enjoy new experiences. Once regarded as an option for only the privileged, gap years can be an opportunity to experience paid work, which will provide an invaluable insight into a range of professions.

Apprenticeships

An apprenticeship is a real job with training, which will enable your child to earn whilst they obtain relevant work skills and study towards a nationally recognised qualification. The apprenticeship must pay at least the national minimum apprenticeship wage but many employers pay significantly more. In addition, there are a number of different financial support schemes available whilst an apprenticeship is being sought and once one has been found.

An apprenticeship takes between one and five years to complete, depending on the apprenticeship level and the industry.

Apprenticeships have not traditionally been viewed as a genuine alternative to university, but the government has recently introduced Degree Apprenticeships as part of the Higher Apprenticeship programme. These provide the opportunity for your child to study for a degree alongside gaining valuable work-based experience—the apprentice will end up with a full Bachelor's or Master's degree without having to meet the cost of a university education.

School leaver programmes

School leaver programmes are similar to Higher Apprenticeships, allowing your son or daughter to gain work-based experience whilst studying part-time usually for a related professional qualification or a degree. They represent an excellent alternative to university for high achieving, motivated and ambitious students. There are various levels of entry requirements but, like Higher and Degree Apprenticeships, are designed to ensure that your child would be at a similar level in their career within two to four years as graduate joiners.

An increasing number of employers have introduced school leaver programmes in recent years, recognising that (especially following the increase in UK university tuition fees in 2012) many talented and motivated school leavers may not wish to go to university and may prefer to enter work immediately. They are popular with banks and accountancy firms, with work experience combined with in-house training and the opportunity to study for a professional qualification or degree alongside. Employers usually build the cost of study into the programme, so your son or daughter would not be facing c. £50,000 of debt at the end of their studies and, in fact, would be earning throughout. Salaries are generally good, reflective of the industries which favour these programmes, with some school leavers starting on a salary in excess of £20,000 per annum.

Sponsored degrees

Increasingly, companies are offering sponsored degrees, which they have developed in collaboration with universities and professional organisations. This enables them to develop graduates who they know will be highly trained in skills relevant to their roles and will be familiar with the company's business. Typically, recruits will have a traditional university experience as full-time students and will enjoy paid work experience and training with the company during holiday periods or part-time. In this way, they will have the opportunity to put the skills they have learned in the classroom into practice in the workplace. Sponsored degree schemes can involve or lead to permanent employment on graduation and at the very least will provide your son or daughter with a significant competitive advantage, having built up a considerable amount of work experience as well as a university degree. In some cases, these programmes also include the completion of a professional qualification, e.g. the PwC Flying Start Degree Programme includes a professional chartered accountancy qualification. In addition, the sponsor will usually pay a proportion of the university tuition and living expenses. Therefore, with salary and benefits your child is likely to complete their degree largely debt free and will potentially secure a graduate level position straight after university.

Your son or daughter will need to be satisfied with their career choice, as there are limited opportunities available. In addition, many programmes are linked to a particular university so there will be restricted choice in terms of the location of study.

Drama schools and music colleges

Although Drama and Music can be studied as academic subjects at universities, those aspiring to careers in music or the theatre may be attracted to one of the specialist colleges with their greater emphasis on practical training. Application systems vary: they can be through UCAS, UCAS Conservatoires or directly to the college / school. The balance between practical and academic work also varies, and thorough research is advisable to meet the precise demands of your child. Competition is tough and gaining a place will involve one or more auditions. An alternative route into the professions is to apply after having completed a university undergraduate degree elsewhere: given the unpredictability of success in the performing arts, it can be good to have a conventional degree to one's credit.

Art school

Increasingly, universities providing degree courses in Fine Art and related subjects often either require or prefer an Art Foundation course to be completed prior to undergraduate study. Art schools provide the opportunity to enhance existing skills and explore new media. Similarly, students interested in pursuing their art studies often choose to take an Art Foundation course.

Alternative study options

While your child may not be ready to commit to an undergraduate degree course, neither may they be confident about a career choice at this early stage in their lives. A foundation degree (usually a one-year course) may provide a good alternative, allowing them to study and gain a qualification but for only 12 months. A foundation degree can then be used to pursue an undergraduate degree if your son or daughter decides that university level study suits them. Having an additional qualification after a year will enhance their academic profile if they decide to enter the workplace.

Alternatively there are a range of professional skills courses, which will provide your son or daughter with valuable transferable skills to prepare them for employment. Many of these course providers will have established links with employers, which will provide excellent opportunities for placements and potential longer term employment.

Employment

Of course, your son or daughter may prefer to go straight into employment but, in order to enhance their longer-term prospects, they may wish to combine this with some part-time study. The Open University provides the opportunity for flexible distance learning study to degree and post-graduate levels, which can be combined with full-time employment and at a lower cost than many traditional university degrees. ■

INDEX

Other titles in The Parent Brief series

Aiming High

Critical thinking skills to help my child fulfil their potential
Debra Price

How can you help your child stand out and succeed in highly competitive environments?

Critical thinking is a skill that will boost their performance in interviews, exams and beyond—for the whole of their life. It's the difference between merely answering questions and really solving problems: an ability that will allow your child to shine and ultimately to maximise their potential.

- **Practical advice on how to encourage your child to think critically**
- **How to make decisions, argue convincingly and make the best impression on interviewers, exam boards and (later) employers**
- **Packed with insider information from the experts: interviewers at independent schools**
- **Checklists and real-life tips from parents who have already been through it**

ISBN 978-0-946095-2-8

School in the UK

The essential guide to my child's education
Victoria Barker

The UK education system is complex and confusing. What do you need to know to make the right decisions for your child's education from start to finish? This indispensable guide gives you straightforward explanations of the milestones and the options available at each stage, helping you to navigate your child's path through school with confidence and ease. From key stages to free schools, from sibling rules to home schooling, we shed light on the mysterious, cut through the red tape and give you honest advice in an easy-to-digest format.

- **Expert advice on choosing your child's educational path and getting the best from the system**
- **Inside information from teachers and heads across a broad range of UK schools**
- **Practical checklists and real-life tips from parents who have already been through it**

ISBN 978-0-946095-71-1

Independent School Entrance

Getting my child into the right school from pre-prep to 6th form
Victoria Barker

You want to send your child to an independent school. Where do you go for the best advice?

This accessible guide gives you all the information you need to make an informed choice and support your child through the application process. We've gathered together expert advice, case studies and tips from other parents to give you a complete overview in one easy-to-use handbook.

- **How to choose and apply to an independent school**
- **Beyond league tables and prospectuses, advice on everything from choosing a school to financial aid and acing the interview**
- **Packed with checklists and real-life tips from parents who have already gone through it**

ISBN 978-0-946095-59-9

For more information and free advice visit **theparentbrief.com**